TESTING
THE NATIONAL
COVENANT

TESTING THE NATIONAL COVENANT

Fears and Appetites in American Politics

William F. May

GEORGETOWN UNIVERSITY PRESS/WASHINGTON, DC

Library of Congress Cataloging-in-Publication Data
May, William F.
Testing the national covenant : fears and appetites in American politics /
William F. May.
p. cm.
Includes bibliographical references and index.
ISBN 978-1-58901-765-8 (case : alk. paper)
1. Consensus (Social sciences)—United States.   2. Public interest—
United States.   3. Common good.   4. Political culture—Moral and
ethical aspects—United States.   5. United States—Politics
and government—2009- I. Title.
JC328.2.M39 2011
306.20973—dc22
2010040836

15 14 13 12 11   9 8 7 6 5 4 3 2
First printing
Printed in the United States of America

For Beverly

CONTENTS

ACKNOWLEDGMENTS

James Billington, director of the Library of Congress, honored me with the Cary M. Maguire and Ann Maguire Chair in Ethics and American History at the John W. Kluge Center at the Library of Congress for the fall of 2007. That grant generously supported studies and a public lecture at the Library titled "Containing Runaway Fears in American Foreign Policy." The topic evolved into the first chapter of this book. Iain Torrance, the president of Princeton Theological Seminary, invited me to deliver the five Levi P. Stone Lectures at the seminary from October 5 to 8, 2009. Dr. Nancy Duff, social ethics professor at the seminary, graciously hosted that occasion, and Professor Richard Amesbury of the Claremont School of Theology offered helpful critical comments. The series of lectures, titled "Testing the National Covenant: Containing Runaway Fears and Appetites," allowed me to lay out the basic direction of this manuscript. Richard Brown, director of Georgetown University Press, encouraged me, as I prepared the Stone Lectures, to plan their eventual publication. A much earlier Guggenheim Fellowship and more recent years spent as the founding director of the Cary M. Maguire Center for Ethics and Public Responsibility at Southern Methodist University encouraged me to move into territory beyond earlier academic interests. At the kind invitation of James Childress, I have been, since 2003, a fellow of the Institute for Practical Ethics at the University of Virginia. My thanks go to all of the above who have provided me with support, expectations, and important deadlines. Peter Weatherly and Donna Packard have rescued me in the final preparation of this manuscript from the mysteries and mixed blessing of my computer.

I am particularly grateful to Cary M. Maguire for his extended personal interest and support for my work. William Lee Miller, Charles E. Curran, George Telford, Jeffrey Maletta, and Ted and David May have read parts of this manuscript and sustained me in other ways. I am indebted to still others over the years. They know who they are. As one such friend and colleague, Tom Mayo of the Southern Methodist University Law School, put it, "thanks" is too small a word. It is immeasurably so in honoring my wife, Beverly, to whom I dedicate this book.

PREFACE

When pollsters and campaign consultants examine the role of religion in politics, they usually have in mind institutional religion. They band the legs of Protestants, Catholics, Jews, Muslims, and Buddhists and observe how they vote. That study is very important. However, this book does not examine the political behavior of individuals identified with official religious traditions. Instead, it explores the primordial religious passions that shape the vision, limit the choices, and ritualize the rhetoric of the political movements themselves. These powerful political movements may be quite unofficial, nontraditional, and even antitraditional religiously; nevertheless, religion can animate their passions and supply them with their shaping narratives.

Religious dualism, for example, has basically defined the radical right in its reaction to the anxieties of the Cold War and to the later threat of terrorism. Religious dualism has also mapped out the cultural landscape of the nation into a war between the heartland and the two coasts—Main Street vs. Hollywood, Washington, DC, and Wall Street. The ideological struggle of absolute good and evil traces all the way back to the Manichaean dualists of the third century and still earlier to the Zoroastrian dualists of the ancient Middle East. These narratives maintain their hold on the human psyche not through the continuities of historical transmission, but through the perennial attractiveness of a story line that interprets human life dyadically as a struggle between absolute good and absolute evil. Dualism is irrepressible. It shows up in the daily life of workers. While the organizational chart of a corporation formally arranges superiors and subordinates into the tidy geometry of a pyramid, workers rearrange things into some of the internal struggles of "us vs. them." Dualism chronically tempts any society that wearies of the complexities and compromises of politics and seeks to substitute for politics the apparent clarities of battle.

In the West, dualism has also nested persistently in the three great Abrahamic traditions of Judaism, Christianity, and Islam. These three monotheistic traditions affirm one God, not two, and recognize that all human beings, friends as well as foes, fall short of God's glory. But the language of monotheism—God vs. satan—is susceptible to a melodramatic reordering that inflates the devil into God's coequal and organizes believers obsessively around the struggle against evil that is equated with their enemies. The historian of religion Frederic Spiegelberg aptly referred to Manichaeism as the most persistent and alive religion in the West and in parts of the world touched by the West: "To many it may appear a dead religion, and as an organized religion it is. But it has millions of followers who have never heard of Mani and who do not even know the nature of the thing they follow."[1] Political movements that are effectively dualistic have sought aggressively for support from various adherents of traditionally monotheistic faiths and indeed have sought to pull the traditions themselves away from their own animating visions.

In my judgment, these political movements and their shaping ideologies cannot be reduced to religious factors alone, as though religion operated in each case as a sole and sufficient cause, exclusive of economic, political, and cultural factors. However, these political movements are underestimated and misunderstood—to the detriment of our national life—when we fail to examine the religious passions that energize them or the religious patterns and narratives to which their basic convictions conform. Impressed with the power of dualism in American politics, Richard Hofstadter examined in 1965 the extremists on the right under the title *The Paranoid Style in American Politics.*[2] However, the leaders of the movement were not clinically paranoid. As Hofstadter himself recognized, the Right had objective grounds for some of its fears; a conspiratorial interpretation of events is not inevitably wrong. In a review of Hofstadter's book in 1966, I proposed instead the title *Manichaeism in American Politics* as a more apt way of exposing the dualism that drove the radical Right in foreign and domestic policy.[3]

This book begins by examining religious patterns and energies at work in foreign and domestic policy on the current scene: the first, under the aspect of fear; the second, under the aspect of desire. The first chapter attends to containing runaway fear in American foreign policy. Fear tempted the United States to defect from its identity as a republic and adopt an imperial agenda: first in the Cold War and then in the war against terrorism. At its worst, this aggressive agenda brooked few limits in its ambition to dominate the world economically and militarily. Alternatively, the government pursued (irregularly) a policy of containment in its dealings with the Soviets. The diplomat and foreign policy analyst George F. Kennan, who helped shape the latter policy, recognized that containing the Soviets, first and foremost, required America's own self-containment, a disciplining of its fears, in order for America to sustain its own identity as a republic in the course of its response to imperial threat. This need for self-containment reappeared as an issue in the later response to terrorism.

The second and third chapters deal with the imperial overreach of free market ideology in domestic policy. Free market ideologues, in their ascendancy, resisted most government restrictions on business through taxes or federal regulations (chapter 2). They also sought to co-opt or marginalize other possible centers of public power—whether the professions, labor unions, universities, religious congregations, or the media (chapter 3). The only regulation that free marketeers embraced as legitimate was self-regulation, which in practice meant too little regulation or none at all.

The fourth chapter deals explicitly with another dynamic in American policies. Whereas the word "imperial" highlights policies that would attempt to banish fear through domination and control, the phrase "runaway appetites" examines personal life and policies that issue from a chronic hunger, a perceived sense of lack. Moreover, a hunger that never abates can drive the effort to overreach. The economist John Maynard Keynes sought to restrain this damaging overreach by proposing a countercyclical fiscal policy that would contain runaway desire in good times (partly through taxes) and counter runaway anxiety and distrust in bad times (partly through public investments). Chapter 4 focuses chiefly on the ceaseless quest for oil that helped drive the American economy for the last one hundred years and that continues to expose the dangerous interplay of desire and anxiety in sustaining the American way of life.

The use of the term "runaway" implies that the root problem in both foreign and domestic policy is not fear or desire as such. Both fear and desire are natural to the human condition, as natural as the threats that beset us and the goods that stir our desires. No political arrangement can wholly ignore the need for security against threats or the provision of goods that serve human survival and flourishing. The root problem is *runaway* fear and appetite, not fear and appetite themselves.

The theological tradition of the West offers background on this issue. The classical Catholic tradition helps recognize and explain the power of desire or appetite in human life and the importance of ordering it. The Protestant tradition lays bare the power of fear or anxiety in human life and the importance of disciplining it. Both traditions also examine the dangerous interplay of fear and desire. Swollen appetites (and egos) can heighten fears of evils that visit from abroad or that threaten at home; they seem to justify an imperious response. Inflated fears can distort, dwindle, or exhaust the goods needed to sate the appetites.

To complicate matters, it is not obvious either to a society or to individuals that their behavior is runaway or out of control. They engage in self-deception. The issue is distorted reasoning, not simply fateful passions. The controlling, authoritarian husband does not think of himself as unreasonable in his demands on his spouse. On the contrary, he perceives her behavior as erratic and out of control. It is she who fails to live up to the script, whose behavior justifies his jailhouse rules and his strict punishment. The controlling husband does not recognize that his controlling behavior is out of control. Similarly, a society quickly naturalizes its excessive appetites. Although its indulgences apparently jut out for all to see—its oil addictions, its stock market run-ups—it can fiercely deny the reach of its ruinous appetites. Such complications will surface in the first four chapters, beginning with fear and imperial ambition in American foreign policy and then turning to the mechanisms of imperious desire in both our foreign and domestic policies.

Together, these four chapters strike a recurrent theme: the inadequacy of a contractualist understanding of American identity in dealing with either our appetites or our fears. A purely contractualist interpretation of America traces our origins as a nation to an agreement based on self-interest alone. That view does not provide much ground for disciplining the self's appetites and fears. It yields too much to the marketplace in ordering our appetites, and until recently it has narrowed too much the role of government to the task of quelling a specific set of fears. The social contract restricts government chiefly to the business of securing our survival against foreign invasion and internal threats of violence. It dismisses the government's further positive role and responsibility to the common good. As the preamble to the Constitution puts it: "to promote the general Welfare."

The last part of the book identifies four basic ways of interpreting identity that bear on the American scene—unnatural, natural, contractual, and covenantal. Only Native Americans and African Americans suffered the violent or *unnatural* imposition of an identity, by conquest or enslavement. However, the plurality in the origins of European immigrants made it difficult for them to affirm a *natural* identity. Americans seem to be one out of many—*e pluribus unum*—not simply one by nature or blood. This book therefore concentrates on the third and fourth ways of interpreting American identity: *contractual* and *covenantal*. These two competing accounts of our origin and prospect as a people figure prominently in the country's founding. Their influential narratives resemble one another in that they both focus on a promise. However, the promises also differ.

A social contract account of the promise reflects the familiar history of negotiated deals struck by self-interested parties. It describes much that goes on in the economic life of the country across the 150 years prior to the founding and shows through in the deliberations that led to the final framework to which the founders signed their names in 1787. A promise constructs a reality out of the multiples of self-interest.

However, a covenantal account of the promissory event differs in that it recognizes the promise as a response to a reality already incipiently there. The Constitution begins with this reality at the very top of the first sentence in the preamble; it purportedly serves as the agent of the promise that follows. The document does not begin with a plurality or an aggregate of self-interested parties. It begins not with "We the individuals" or "We the interest groups" or "We the factions" but with "We the People." The people are already there as a given: not simply as a given in the sense of something that individuals are stuck with, but as a gift, an imperfect gift, upon which the people now build. This gift does not appear out of thin air. It presupposes a history of mutual giving and receiving—and bearing with one another—spread across 150 years in the midst of all that buying and selling prior to the founding. The answering promise deepens the bond and alters the future of the people covenanting among themselves. It recognizes a deeper source and a wider horizon for the business of buying and selling that has transpired in their life together. The answering promise and disciplined framework would sustain and improve the people's continuance and flourishing as they proceed now to form a "more perfect union." The concept of a covenant holds together a doubleness in the American identity of gift and task. The nation is both a community and a community in the making.

The biblical narrative of God's covenant with the people and of their covenants with one another, including gift and response to gift, appears over and over again in the 150-year experience of the American settlers prior to the founding. The theological aspect of the narrative—God, the granter—did not directly inspire the language of those who drafted the Constitution. They were not theologians or, for the most part, churchgoers. During the ebb and flow of church life from the 1740s to 1860 (an era that included three great waves of revivals), institutional religion during the general period of the founding ebbed more than it flowed.

The Declaration of Independence appeals to the laid-back God of deism, not to the energetic God of biblical theism. Piety does not resound in the preamble to the Constitution or in any of the prosaic compromises that found their way into the body of the document. The word "religion" does not appear in the main document at all. It finally surfaces in the Bill of Rights, where the crafters of the First Amendment made a point of banning the establishment of religion, either in a generalized form or in the form of any particular denomination.

Still, a covenantal sensibility supplies part of the soil from which the Constitution emerges. The preamble celebrates the blessings of liberty. Moreover, the liberties soon inscribed in the First Amendment are not the private liberties of individualism that would shrink the public space in which the people might pursue their common good. On the contrary, the First Amendment promptly singles out a cluster of liberties that are civil liberties. The several liberties of speech, assembly, press, and religion reassure and invite citizens to move out of the burrow of private preference and into public places where they can gather, debate, and resolve issues in pursuit of the common good.

Thus, while leaders invoked the word "freedom" more often than any other word at the time of the revolution, the second most often invoked term was "public virtue," a phrase they defined as the readiness to sacrifice self-interest to the common good. The revolutionaries recognized that, not only during the exigency of war but in the republic to follow, liberty would not long survive unless in its exercise people were ready to make some sacrifices for the common good. The revolutionaries drew their language about public virtue from the more communitarian wing of the Enlightenment, but this appeal struck a cord with a people who, from their first shipboard covenant through 150 years of experience in self-governance, required some measure of self-expenditure in service to the common good. Through the ordeal of the Civil War and beyond, the still-developing nation required the disciplined containment of its runaway fears and appetites in the course of sustaining its national identity.

That sense of national identity is currently being tested in both the foreign and domestic policies of the United States. Contractual and covenantal accounts of national identity deal differently with unruly appetites and fears in both areas. This book wrestles throughout its pages with these issues. It closes, however, with the resurgence today of the question of identity for this immigrant nation with the arrival and treatment of some twelve million undocumented workers. The issue rankles in the border states but also flares out irregularly on the national stage. In traditional meaning the word "covenant" affirmed a bond between people that goes deeper than the more superficial and transient tie of a contract. However, this deeper alteration of identity can be dangerous. Does it arise as a bond solely to wall out the stranger—like a real estate covenant or a tacit agreement in our residentially segregated churches? Does the covenant of a nation, itself composed of immigrants, collapse incoherently upon the terms of its own founding?

The book closes with an attempt to address that question, but first it turns to those runaway fears that have sorely tested national identity in shaping American foreign policy.

1

CONTAINING RUNAWAY FEARS IN
AMERICAN FOREIGN POLICY

This cautionary tale recounts the religious apprehensions embedded in American politics, especially in our foreign policy after World War II, as the country dealt anxiously with the successive threats of global tyranny and anarchy. I am a Christian theologian, not a political theorist. Why would I venture into this topic since I am not a political leader, a consultant to leaders, or an op-ed critic of leaders? Niccolò Machiavelli gives encouragement here. In his letter dedicating *The Prince* to Lorenzo the Magnificent, Machiavelli asked why anyone would dare to give advice to princes who was not himself a prince working the high ground. He compared himself to a landscape painter who views the mountains from the advantage of a distance that might cast a fresh light on governance.[1]

The scriptures of Israel, although some 2,500 years distant from the current scene, cast light on a world beset by the twin threats of tyranny and anarchy. The First Book of Samuel (8:10–18), a narrative about the first rulers of Israel, warns against the fundamental social evil of tyranny. The people hanker for a king to protect them, but the prophet warns that a king will rule arbitrarily and unjustly. The Book of Judges, recording an earlier time of scattered tribes, flags the opposite social evil of anarchy: "In those days there was no king in Israel; every man did what was right in his own eyes" (21:25).[2] In one way or another, every society struggles with the twin social evils of tyranny (a form of injustice) and anarchy. These evils pair with two basic and sometimes contending social goods:

1

justice and order. Every society needs some measure of order to stave off chaos, and it hopes for rulers who will exercise their ordering power justly.

The founders of the United States wrestled with the balance between these two contending social goods or, more pointedly, with the paired social evils that were identified twenty-five centuries earlier. As revolutionaries they opposed, in the first instance, the tyrant King George. No less urgently the founders of the nation, following the failure of their first attempt in the Articles of Confederation, also sought to thwart the anarchy that would befall a newly independent nation, should each colony simply do what it deemed right in its own eyes.

Thus the founders devised a Constitution that would contain runaway fear. They recognized that an unbounded fear of tyranny would let a society slide into anarchy: hence the need for an energetic and effective federal government. However, a runaway fear of anarchy might produce tyranny: hence the need for a government with built-in checks and balances in the exercise of its power.[3]

Building a just and well-ordered society is no easy task, then or now. Campaigning against injustice alone, reformers can throw the established order into turmoil. Enforcing solely established order, a dominant leadership can ignore injustices and oppress.

In striking a balance, wise leaders recognize both social goods. No one campaigned more persistently on behalf of those deprived of injustice than Martin Luther King Jr. However, his "Letter from Birmingham City Jail" detailed a strategy for civil disobedience that also respected order. (King insisted that his followers negotiate with their opponents before engaging in disobedience, exercise discipline to keep their disobedience nonviolent, and disobey only as a last resort, and even then with the final intent of resuming negotiations.) Meanwhile, his opponents regularly invoked the good of order, but some of them wisely came to realize that a failure to remedy injustice could undercut the stability they prized.

Such progressives and conservatives differ dramatically as to which good they rank primary and which secondary. However, to the degree that they recognize both social goods, they occupy the "left" and the "right" within a common arena of political discourse. Radicals on the right and left differ from such centrists in that they rashly organize themselves solely around the good they prize and against the evil they fear.[4]

RELIGIOUS DUALISM AND ANXIETY FACING TYRANNY

The evils described in biblical times have followed us into the modern era. After World War II the leading political anxiety in foreign policy focused on the evil of global tyranny. Most Americans (not only those on the political right) believed that a totalitarian state, the Soviet empire, endangered Europe and eventually the United States of America. In its extreme form this anxiety supported an unconditional arms race against a country whose conventional forces exceeded our own. The Soviets mirrored this anxiety in reverse, as they maneuvered against the military and economic colossus of the West. Meanwhile the very powers of mass destruction that each side wielded to oppose the enemy it feared generated further fears. The opposing superpowers, edgy with nuclear weapons, could—either by accident, by runaway fear, or by malice aforethought—destroy one another.

Religiously put, a dualist vision drove extremists in the East and the West.[5] The ancient dualists reduced all distinctions in the universe to the cosmic struggle between two rival powers: the kingdom of God pitted against the kingdom of Satan, Good versus Evil, Light against Darkness, Spirit opposed to Matter. Modern dualists have embedded this cosmic struggle in the arena of politics. After World War II, dualists identified the forces of righteousness with the capitalist West and identified the legions of Satan with the Communist East. The Communists returned the favor by reversing the players in the mythology: the Soviets would usher in the New Jerusalem by vanquishing Western economic imperialism.

In either case, the common term in the Manichæan story line is "kingdom." Each side perceives its enemy as hierarchically organized. In its revolutionary activity the Communist Party did not tolerate the disorderly dabbling of adventurers or badly timed spontaneous uprisings. Correspondingly, the West organized itself hierarchically for the sake of efficiency, both in the military and in the setting of large corporations. The philosopher Alasdair MacIntyre highlighted this common organizational feature of the modern conflict between capitalism and Communism by identifying Max Weber, not Adam Smith or Karl Marx, as the ruling theoretician of the modern world.[6] While differing from each other in their ideological content, the West and the East have mimicked each other in their dominant organizational form—the bureaucracy—of which Weber was the great cartographer.[7]

In their appeal to portions of the electorate in America, dualists have often invoked the language of biblical monotheism—Good versus Evil, God versus Satan. However, monotheism and dualism differ. Monotheists affirm God to be one—not two. Evil is *real* but not *ultimate*. Dualists tend to act as if the devil is coequal to God. They obsessively orient their lives and policies around the ultimate foe. Any limits on their anxieties and rage seem unwarranted and unjustified. Further, by separating humans into two organized, warring camps of the righteous and the unrighteous, dualists dismiss the Pauline warning that all fall short of the glory of God (see Rom 3:23). They are metaphysical separatists. They particularly abhor the confusion, commingling, and tainting of good with evil.[8] They prefer the clarity of military contest (pointed toward a final rollback and victory) to political compromise.

THE CONTAINMENT OF TYRANNY

Under President Harry S Truman, the United States developed a response to the threat of the Soviets not by acting on the dualist script from the political right, but rather by following—irregularly—the more moderate policies of deterrence and containment (and the rebuilding of Europe) spearheaded by Secretary of State George C. Marshall and Undersecretary Dean Acheson. They drew heavily on proposals developed by George F. Kennan, the *charge d'affaires* of the US mission in the Soviet Union and at length the head of the policy planning staff in the State Department. Kennan argued for the diplomatic and military containment of the expansionist tendencies of America's former ally. Containment required recognizing the evil of tyranny for what it is but at the same time putting it in the lower case, not exaggerating it by capitalizing it. Militarily, containment excluded both appeasing the Soviets and seeking supremacy over them.

Less noticeably, Kennan emphasized that containing the Soviets required that the United States contain itself and its own insecurities. The United States should not view the Soviet Union through the distortions of fear, as though the enemy were indelibly powerful and evil. An anxious overreaction to Soviet tyranny was unjustified and could be self-defeating. It would succeed merely in draining American resources needed for long-term competition and arouse animosities against us elsewhere. Kennan reminded us that we see "as if through a glass darkly" (1 Cor 13:12). We should not automatically assume that the Soviet Union will remain inalterably what it is, unless defeated by American military misadventures. Kennan's hope rested on something more substantial than the vague feeling that maybe something better would turn up later. An overextended imperial Soviet Union, he believed, could not sustain itself indeterminately into the future.

Kennan also believed that an anxious overreaction to the Soviets would be self-deforming for the United States. It would alter the American republic into a hypertensive empire. Containment of the Soviet Union required America's own self-containment. Long-term competition required that America remain firmly and patiently what it is, a republic: "The most important influence that the United States can bring to bear upon internal developments in Russia will continue to be the influence of example; the influence of what it is, and not only what it is to others but what it is to itself."[9] The United States should refrain from bossy report card keeping and moralizing in its dealings with the Soviets and other nations. Self-containment called for a brace of continuing virtues: firmness, patience, humility, self-confidence, and hope.[10]

Forty years later, Kennan's message of patience and hope seemed vindicated by the dramatic events of 1989. In his single-volume sweep of the Cold War the historian John Lewis Gaddis bracketed the period with an opening chapter on the "return of fear" (the insecurities besetting the victors at the end of World War II) and closed with a final chapter on the "triumph of hope" (as the imperial Soviet Union devolved into the diminished Russia of 1989).[11] Clearly the Cold War had not been entirely cold. Wars were fought in east and southeast Asia, and small nations were crushed. However, no nuclear weapons were dropped, and the great powers had not directly engaged in battle. Gaddis argued that Kennan was vindicated.

Politically, however, the story did not end entirely in a triumph of hope. A second and differing wave of anxiety overran the major players in the later stages of the Cold War and dampened any disposition to celebrate unalloyed hope in either the East or the West: the threat of anarchy.

ANARCHY ON THE CURRENT SCENE

The Soviets experienced first, and most traumatically, a shift in their anxieties toward the threat of anarchy. Although glasnost and perestroika opened up the Soviet empire to the outside world, the society quickly spun out of control as client states and regions within the Soviets broke off from the empire. The government suffered a chronic hemorrhaging of its resources in Afghanistan and a decade later in Chechnya. Authorities sold off public assets of the nation at fire sale prices, creating economic warlords who ran their fiefdoms as they pleased. The earlier meltdown at Chernobyl had laid waste to an entire region and came to symbolize the plight of a society that had lost the ability to contain explosive powers within.

At length a similar but subtler shift in political anxieties appeared in the West. Iraq's invasion of Kuwait threatened the stability of a world order that depended upon both oil and the territorial integrity of nation-states, and a rash of troubles broke out in the 1990s. "Failed nations" became a category in political thought. Cumulatively, the disintegration of the Balkans, the implosions in Africa, the flare-ups between the Arabs and Israelis—and, most spectacularly, on a clear, blue, telegenic day that we now call "9/11," the towering symbols of prevailing power for the United States, the "commanding heights" as it were, fell to the ground, Ground Zero. Thereafter a second religious vision offered a different narrative account of the political scene: not order versus malevolent order, but order versus chaos, the political term for which is "anarchy."

THE BABYLONIAN CREATION MYTH

From the 1990s forward the nation has been moving from the basic story line of Manichæan dualism to a narrative that can be traced back to dualist scriptures older than the Book of Genesis. The Babylonian creation myth gives an account of a cosmic struggle between two rival gods: not order versus malevolent order this time, but rather order versus chaos. Marduk, a kind of sheriff deity and the enforcer of law and order, battles Tiamat, a formless monster issuing from turbulent waters, the symbol of primordial chaos. Marduk slays Tiamat and fashions the world out of Tiamat's dismembered body (and humankind out of the blood of Tiamat's son, who contrived the uprising against order). Thus the world we know and the creatures we are participate, at the same time, in both order and chaos.

To complicate the picture: Marduk has a taste for violence. He not only slays but dismembers Tiamat's body. He is given to a somewhat enthusiastic overkill. Thorkild Jacobson discerned that an "element of wildness and violence" issues from the inner depths of the god of order.[12] The myth reminds us that a society threatened with disruption and chaos may suspend its self-restraints and rally around its police and militia for the sake of law and order. It may even tolerate an outcropping of lawlessness in its law enforcers, permitting them a kind of frenzy and ecstasy in protecting the compound of the law. One tribe in Africa referred to its lawless defenders as "the king's knives." The king let them stand outside of the law while making their stand for the law.[13] The mythic contest does not offer a perfectly pure conflict of opposites. Although at first glance the struggle seems a clear-cut battle between rival symbols— Marduk versus Tiamat, law and order versus chaos—the dragon's tail may show beneath the sheriff's uniform.

The Babylonian creation myth expresses a dread of chaos through the image of floods that engulf and overwhelm all structures and forms. The periodic flooding of the two great rivers of Mesopotamia may have inspired the ancient myth. Tiamat roils in the flood waters.[14] In our time we have experienced the shudder of chaos in Babylon itself and on our own gulf shores after Hurricane Katrina.[15]

TERRORISM AND THE THREAT OF ANARCHY

Disarray in distant places did not seize the United States with as much anxiety as that singularly violent event that seemed to split time in two—September 11, 2001. The terrorists aimed at the supreme symbols of the "new world order" (the phrase of the day) for shaping the future after the breakup of the Soviet Union. The first target, the World Trade Center, symbolized (and claimed by name) an economic ascendancy over the world located in New York City. The second target, the Pentagon, symbolized the very heart of the modern West's account of the origin and justification for the state. From the seventeeth century forward, the West, following social contract theory, traced the origins of the state not to a supreme good—God or the sacrifice of a founding hero—but to the protection the state provides against a supreme evil—the evils of theft, invasion, and violent death. We give to the state a monopoly over the power of death, authorizing its police and military powers; and in exchange the government assures us that when we go to sleep we will not be robbed or murdered in the night. That is the political deal. People fear death and so they enter into a contract, conveying to the state the awesome power to kill in order that they may not be killed.[16]

However, the terrorist event proclaims on television that the state cannot protect us against a violent death. The terrorist breaks the state's monopoly over violence, not simply by the terrorist's readiness to kill but by his or her willingness to die. Wrapped in explosives, the terrorist stands outside of ordinary fear and therefore the power of the state. The terrorist is an ecstatic in the literal sense of that word. Meanwhile, the rest of us, who still fear death, have lost our protector. Decades ago, when the Irish conflict erupted in the bombing of various pubs in London, a member of parliament said, "From now on, every man, his own magistrate." Scotland Yard cannot protect us. Random violence suffuses the everyday with uncertainty and therefore with the prospect of the anarchic.

In their choice of means—the commercial airplane—the terrorists on September 11 also denied to Americans the comfort of believing we are safe at a distance. Anybody can be on an airplane. There is no longer any security in obscurity or anonymity. Television moreover guarantees that the event, caught on camera, will annihilate distance and reverberate liturgically over and over again in the country.

The attacks of terrorists were ecstatic in the further sense that they did not seem to fit into the sequential world of political means and ends. Why did they do it? To what purpose? What did they hope to accomplish by a propaganda of deed? Their actions seemed only to galvanize hatred and fear.

In the past, critics tended to interpret terrorist movements simply as a type of political strategy and found them wanting. They were counterproductive and self-destructive. As John Hume, a Catholic member of Parliament, once put it, "The Provos bombed themselves to the conference table, and then they bombed themselves away again."[17] So interpreted, terrorist action breaks up into what Hannah Arendt called the irrational.[18] The connections between means and ends and between agent, victim, and intended social consequence so attenuate that the action juts out as absurd. It becomes a politically impenetrable end in itself.[19]

Ecstatic events may transcend political strategy at the level of means and ends but reintroduce politics at another level. Although they break with the conventional notion of a politics of effectiveness that leads to the conference table, they offer what Weber and John Yoder, in other settings, have called a politics of witness. Endlessly repeated episodes of violence seem to signal the passing of the apparently fixed world and to herald something else aborning. Their politics of witness aspire to return to a "ground zero."

In response, any government seeking to stop terrorism also seems to slide into the irrational and counterproductive. Its actions lose connection to the causal nexus of means and ends. Its overreaction is difficult to curtail, even though it solves no problem. By discharging a boundless resentment, the government yields only an immediate satisfaction. It offers enticingly an immediate end in itself, but no future.

In the first stage of the American reaction to the attack of 9/11, American leaders seemed aware of the problem of shaping the future. President George W. Bush emphasized the importance of humility and the fair treatment of Muslims in his address to a joint session of Congress on September 20, 2001. He soon reversed his earlier dismissive 2000 campaign talk against nation building and recognized the necessity of reconstruction in Afghanistan following the overthrow of the Taliban government.

In the course of 2002, however, leaders shifted attention (and funding) from Afghanistan to the prospect of a preventive strike against Iraq for reasons and purposes that kept changing and expanding. Critics warned that in going to war against Iraq, the United States risked becoming the source of destabilizing power in the Middle East and the world at large and also risked becoming conflicted in its own interior life. In dismay General Anthony Zinni—former commander in chief of the United States Central Command, in charge of all troops in the Middle East—later complained that, in fighting Iraq, America struck a beehive with a baseball bat.[20] Therewith, we handed Osama bin Laden a great gift. An increasingly marginalized movement managed to expose, to an aroused Muslim world and a baffled Western world, the preeminent power on earth in its relative powerlessness. America's exercise of power seemed self-defeating.

The religious story line embedded in the administration's response to 9/11 was puzzling. The Bush administration declared that the attack changed the world, yet the government failed to respond to the distinctive threat of anarchy that terrorism posed. Its rhetoric and policies still conformed to a pre-9/11 mindset. It relied on the old diagnostic category of order pitted against malevolent political order, rather than order versus chaos. The administration viewed its enemy as the old recognizable nation-state even though, as it later came to realize, its terrorist opponents were politically amorphous and transnational. Meanwhile, the nation of Iraq supplied all the combustible human materials for an eructing chaos. The government quickly turned its guns on Iraq after invading Afghanistan and identified three governments as constituting an "axis of evil," a phrase that attempted to carry forward the old organizing principle for fighting World War II.

At first, the administration campaigned against al-Qaeda itself as if it were hierarchically organized. It used that most convenient symbol of hierarchy—a deck of cards—to identify and rank each of al-Qaeda's leaders and display to the media its progress in defeating the movement. However, bin Laden and Ayman al-Zawahiri do not control terrorism like the chair of the board and the CEO of General Motors. Terrorist groups operate somewhat more like do-it-yourselfers and decentralized franchises than a bureaucracy that might be wholly defeated from the top down. While unitary in spirit, the terrorists do not depend upon unitary control.

Bin Laden did not aspire to take territorial control of a government like the revolutionaries or expansionist empires of the past. The old strategic categories of "falling dominos" or government takeovers did not quite apply to the struggles in the Middle East. Instead, terrorists in Iraq and elsewhere aimed at turning the strengths of the highly interdependent global order of the West against itself. John Robb in *Brave New War* called this aspect of the basic terrorist strategy "systems disruption."[21] Along with random attacks on people, this strategy inspired selective attacks on the global system in its vulnerabilities—its pipelines, airlines, utilities, electricity supply lines, roads, and communications systems. Meanwhile, the misguided reactions of the United States and other governments produced a phenomenal rate of return for terrorists in their conduct of a poor man's war. Al-Qaeda invested approximately half a million dollars in the attack on 9/11, but it provoked a response from the United States that was climbing toward a trillion dollars by 2008. That figure paled before the immeasurable costs to the United States alone in soldiers killed and injured and damage done to its power position in the world. Meanwhile, the protracted disarray in Iraq altered the conventional metrics of American military and political power.

CONTAINING THE THREAT OF TERRORISM

A foreign policy that would contain the long-term threat of chaos once again calls for containment—a third way between supremacy and appeasement. Ian Shapiro, a Yale political scientist, put it succinctly: "The idea behind containment is to refuse to be bullied while at the same time declining to become a bully."[22]

Critics of containment have objected that terrorists have changed the nature of the game for the nation-state. Conventional tactics will no longer work. The political irrationality of terrorism demolishes the traditional diplomatic ploys of restraining bullies with disincentives and incentives. How can one contain or deter terrorists with the prospect of death when they have already handed themselves over to martyrdom?

Shapiro responded to this challenge by distinguishing between three groups: the attackers, their leaders, and the leaders of enabling states.[23] Although the attackers (whom I have described as ecstatic) may not be eliminable and all their attacks may not be deterrable, they are containable. Terrorists do not attack without aid. Even if individual terrorists operate at a level indifferent to death, their leaders and enabling institutions and states will be susceptible to incentives and disincentives for the sake of the survival of their cause or their community.

What are the long-term prospects for containment today? In assessing Islam an argument can be made that the prospects are at least as good for a favorable outcome today as Kennan could reasonably have hoped for in the contest with the Soviets. Admittedly terrorists draw on some passages in the Qur'an to justify their cause. However, the diversity within the sacred scriptures and traditions of Islam give as much or more ground for hope in the emergence of moderating influences in Islam than the writings of Marx, Vladimir Lenin, and Joseph Stalin justified hope for changes in the Soviets and worldwide Communism.

However, even more intensively in this case, the United States must recognize that containment calls for self-containment. To contain itself the nation needs a better sense of what power is and what the role of the country is in its exercise. This recognition requires that the nation not yield to runaway fear and distort itself as a republic or indulge in an imperial presidency or in the fantasies of the imperial self.

THE CONCEPTION AND EXERCISE OF POWER

Despite its floundering in the Middle East, the United States still wields preeminent power in the world today—both hard power and soft. The moralist Albert Camus, in *The Rebel*, wryly distinguished the two kinds of power by observing that power includes not only the force of a tornado but sap in the tree. The violence of shock and awe is one thing; the surge of organic growth, another.

Recently and less vividly, Joseph S. Nye Jr. argued that the hard power of sticks and carrots (military and economic) does not in itself let a country such as the United States sustain its influence or command. The country depends also upon its soft power, which often operates indirectly: the respect of others for its laws and its law-abidingness, the attractiveness of its educational and cultural institutions, its support for international institutions and enduring alliances, and, for better or for worse, the worldwide addictiveness of its technologies and the penetration of its mass media.[24]

Nye's distinction between hard and soft does not hold in some important cases. Ordinarily, economic power beats down like sticks on poor people and nations that have few carrots and little or no bargaining power in dealing with the mighty. However, money can also fertilize the fields of poor nations under more forgiving conditions of loans and investments. Ordinarily, education functions as soft power; however, sometimes it imposes itself on a minority like forced feeding. It gags rather than nourishes, and it produces in a minority what Franz Fanon once called a "spiritual lockjaw."[25]

Ascendant power depends upon a material base from below and a kind of legitimacy from above or from its surround. In addition to much else, successive empires of the West have depended upon the power of wind and water (the Dutch), steam (the British), and oil (the Americans) to drive them militarily and economically.[26] But they have also depended, in varying degrees, upon a kind of legitimacy bestowed upon them by the benefits of protection derived from their hard power and by the communicability of their economic and soft powers.[27] Ascendant powers fail when they have depleted (or failed to adapt or replace) their outmatched material base and when their economic and soft powers seem unsharable or undesirable.

In a world in which no monopoly on the use of force can provide a nation with total security—not even the United States—how should the country conceive its exercise of power in relationship to others? First over others? First apart from others? Or first among equals?

Before the election of George W. Bush in 2000 the neoconservatives strongly backed the doctrine of *first over others*. They argued that the United States as the sole superpower, occupying a "position unmatched since Rome," should not act like a "reluctant sheriff." It should be ready to project power and "conceive of itself as a European power, an Asian power, a Middle Eastern power, and of course, a Western Hemispherean power." Thereby the United States would fulfill its role in sustaining a benevolent global hegemony in a world that has already been transformed economically "in America's image."[28]

Until recently, when Americans looked into the mirror, they did not see an imperial face. They associated the word "empire" with a permanent territorial occupation of other countries. While they would be surprised to know that at least 725 American military bases exist outside the country, they took pride in the United States of America as a nation without ambitions to plant the American flag elsewhere.[29] Meanwhile, decisions made in American boardrooms could alter foreign landscapes, for good or for ill, far more decisively than soldiers showing the British flag in nineteenth-century India.

The Bush administration acted on the doctrine of *first over others*, both before and after 9/11. The government's defense policy called for a military prowess exceeding that of all other nations combined, and it loosened the restraints on using that power to go to war. The administration appeared before the United Nations in the run-up to the war in Iraq only reluctantly and tactically, and it dismissed the warnings from its long-term partners in those alliances as offering the counsel of "old Europe." It replaced the stricter standard of a preemptive war (which allows a nation to attack only in the case of an imminent threat) with the looser standard of a preventive war (which justifies attack in the case of a more vaguely defined "gathering threat"). In effect this looser standard gave leaders the widest possible latitude in taking the country to war and loosened restraints on how they might conduct it. Leaders in the Justice Department passed off some provisions of the Geneva Convention on the abusive treatment of prisoners and torture as quaint and obsolete, and the Defense Department and the CIA acted accordingly.

The old isolationist doctrine of *first apart from others* appealed to Americans in the 1930s and reappeared on the libertarian right and the re-emerging left in their reaction to the long-term policies of George W. Bush and, more recently, to Barack Obama's proposed short-term military commitment to Afghanistan. In a sense, a common thread underlies policies of either domination or withdrawal. By simply withdrawing from the world the United States would repeat a strategy on a global scale that has appealed to some of the privileged within the country—the security of being a gated community. But withdrawal is no longer an option for a country that has undercut—through its transportation, economic, and communication systems, to say nothing of its addiction to oil—its capacity to survive alone. The path of isolationism is also dubious morally. It neither repairs the damages wrought by American hegemony nor discharges the responsibilities that fall upon a nation of ranking power.

The third self-conception, *first among equals,* would recognize America's current preeminent power as a fact of life but attempt to lead rather than to dominate or withdraw from the world. In general direction, an American foreign policy that leads other nations, rather than dominating them, should be multilateral rather than unilateral. It should repair and strengthen its enduring alliances; it should heal, as best it can, botched relations in the Middle East, set the course for its relations to the fast-rising powers of China and India, and mend its frayed relations with international bodies, such as NATO and the United Nations. It should attend seriously to global warming and encourage the development of new, sustainable resources and energies on which human life and flourishing will depend on an overburdened planet. It will also need to respond to the seething expectations that roil modern life, often issuing from the poor, the politically voiceless, and the culturally bereft, which neither passive reliance on the mechanism of globalization nor the all-consuming war on terrorism adequately address.

It is not my purpose in this chapter to examine the important particulars of this third kind of role in foreign policy. I am concerned chiefly with exploring theologically how our anxious response to the external threats of terrorism and tyranny has tempted us to favor the role of dominating rather than leading other nations. No single election retires such issues. Are we a republic or an empire? Does the president operate within a system of checks and balances? Or do the exigencies of our current plight demand a vastly expanded presidential role in foreign policy and domestic security? What view of the citizen, imperial or civic, underlies these debates?

Since recent leaders have used some of the familiar language of monotheism to support their imperial understanding of the nation's mission, the president's authority, and the citizen's identity, comments are in order as Christian thought bears on these issues.

MONOTHEISM, DUALISM, AND
NATIONAL SELF-CONCEPTION

Monotheistic belief calls for a basic conception of the nation and a foreign policy at once humbler and more confident than the religious outlook that has shaped the recently prevailing conception of America's role. Although he is no theologian, Zbigniew Brzezynski touches on the larger scheme of things. There are no immortal nations or empires. "America's global dominance" in the course of time "will fade."[30] That fact should be religiously bearable on the grounds that God, not America, is the beginning and end of all things. However, this powerful but mortal country and its institutions can also leave a legacy in the course of its continuance under wise leadership. Wisdom, however, requires keeping the country's fears and anxieties under control, lest it distort its fundamental identity as a nation.

Biblical realism addresses the issue of fear and anxiety. Monotheism affirms that the evils of both injustice and chaos are real, but not ultimate. We misinterpret and undervalue our lives, our politics, and much else when we split the world asunder into two gods, whether order versus malevolent order or order versus chaos.

Dualists of either sort tend to be religiously grim, and in their apprehensiveness they reach for total control and power. Their language poaches on the messianic. He who is not with us is against us. This mindset speeds the collapse of politics and diplomacy. A foreign policy of runaway fear drives for absolute security, which in turn justifies the unilateral presumption to create an empire. Meanwhile, imperialists in their isolation are prey to the fear that every challenge, every limit, undercuts their control. Thus their insecurity spreads unabated. Presumption and anxiety feed one another, and politics starves. Politics depends upon entrusting and trust-building gestures, which the anxious imperialist who insists on absolute control cannot offer. In this isolation the imperialist cannot suffer any limits on power.

In a culture of fear, leaders and their subordinates, charged with security, are tempted to press beyond the previously accepted limits of the law. For example, Jack Goldsmith, the conservative head of the Office of Legal Council in the Justice Department (2003–4), puzzled over the reasons for the bad judgment of his predecessors in drafting the August 1, 2002, and March 14, 2003, opinions of the department that prepared the way for Abu Ghraib and the torture and abuse of "alien unlawful inhabitants." He surmised, "The main explanation is fear."[31] When Goldsmith reported to Alberto Gonzales, then the president's attorney, and to David Addington, then the vice president's assistant and later his chief of staff, that he could not justify legally an "important terrorist counter-measure," Addington responded in disgust, "If you rule that way, the blood of a hundred thousand people will be on your hands."[32]

In this heated atmosphere Vice President Dick Cheney reportedly argued, "If there is a one percent chance that Pakistani scientists are helping Al Qaeda build or develop a nuclear weapon, we have to treat it as a certainty in terms of our response." Cheney expanded, "It's not about our analysis, or finding a preponderance of evidence. . . . It's about our response."[33] This doctrine justified a policy based on a remote and abstract possibility, not a perceived reality. As the world's only superpower, the neoconservatives urged, the United States should concentrate on creating new realities rather than tethering itself to the realpolitik of old Europe. It need not feel obliged to consider all factors, influences, and consequences of action, as it recreated the Middle East and reconfigured the world.

THE ILLUSIONS OF EMPIRE

In addition to its supply of hard and soft power, a nation needs to respect the importance of what has been recently dubbed "smart power." The currently popular phrase implies a reaction to at least two aggressive ways of being dumb: acting on the illusions of either omniscience or omnipotence. In an aphorism reminiscent of the Christian realist Reinhold Niebuhr, Arthur Schlesinger Jr. once observed, "History is the best antidote to illusions of omnipotence and omniscience."[34] In my judgment the earlier Cold War realists suffered primarily from the illusion of omniscience. Richard Nixon and Henry Kissinger prided themselves in being experts in how the world works. Kissinger warned, "We should not destroy what is possible by forcing events beyond what the circumstances will allow."[35] Statecraft would triumph through their craftiness.

In contrast, the neoconservatives suffered from the illusion of omnipotence while they were in the driver's seat during the invasion of Iraq. They believed that the United States had the power to create the circumstances in Iraq and elsewhere, circumstances to which other nations would have to adjust. The government did not need to know the religious and cultural intricacies of the world it was replacing. In a sense history did not matter. Democracy would follow swiftly upon overthrowing the tyrant. The whole world, Iraq not excepted, thirsts for freedom, defined as we define it.

Classical conservative thinkers as early as Edmund Burke have countered that history does matter. Democracy has to be grown, not simply imposed. As it takes hold it resembles less the tornado than sap in the tree. We need not agree with every detail of Brzezinski's analysis in *Second Chance* to appreciate the importance of organic growth to a democracy: "Democracy historically has emerged through a prolonged process of enhancement of human rights, first from the economic, and then to the political . . . that process in turn entails the progressive appearance of the rule of law, and the gradual imposition of legal and constitutional rules over the structure of power."[36] History warns against the illusion of remaking the world in our own image.[37]

CURBING THE IMPERIAL PRESIDENCY

Recovering our national identity in foreign policy depends upon rebalancing the several branches of government within the United States. Those who define America's role as first over others on the global stage pushed (while they were in office) for a presidency that exerted dominant power over the other branches of government and over the press on the domestic scene. Most particularly

Cheney believed for decades that the nation had suffered a series of events that weakened the president's power at the hands of Congress, the courts, and the press. The Freedom of Information Act and leaks to the press ensnared the presidency of Ronald Reagan in the Iran-Contra affair. Other affronts to presidential power included the appointment of independent councils to investigate and perhaps indict executive officers and staff; and most notably, the Church Committee of the US Senate led to limitations on surveillance with the passage in 1978 of FISA, the Foreign Intelligence Surveillance Act. Cumulatively, presidential power diminished in deference to activist judges and 535 legislators and to the twenty-twenty hindsight of independent councils and op-ed writers for the *New York Times.* Cheney agreed with Caspar Weinberger, former secretary of defense, who stated that "the real world effect often turns out . . . not to be a *transfer* of power from the President to Congress, but a *denial* of power to the government as a whole."[38]

The recovery of presidential power first required secrecy. Cheney's insistence on secrecy was not, in his judgment, a personal cartoonish eccentricity. The executive branch of government needs to get candid advice even in ordinary times on such matters as energy policy without the intrusions and distractions of Congress and the press. After 9/11, policies not only on energy but on immigration, the treatment of prisoners, surveillance, and much else, in his view, belonged under the blanket of security needs. Since the enemy might see patterns in bits of information—however harmless—the government should be able to shut down without explanation the public's right to know.[39]

Meanwhile, conversely, the Bush/Cheney White House insisted on expanding its own right to know. It proceeded with warrantless wiretapping (and with nondisclosure of noncompliance) on the grounds that neither Congress nor the courts could constrain the president in fulfilling his duty. So urgent was the duty to protect the nation's security that the president could suspend treaty restraints and the country's Uniform Code of Military Justice in obtaining information from unlawful combatants without pursuing authorization for these prohibited activities from Congress and the courts. In fact, pursuing authorization would be a mistake, even if one had good reason to know that approval would be forthcoming.

It would concede too much to Congress and the courts, as though the power was theirs in the first instance. Thus, the right to know and the right not to be known were vested in the president's office. Sealed off from the constraints of the Geneva Convention, Congress, and the courts, the president's accountability would effectively narrow to quadrennial elections.

In further expanding presidential power the Bush/Cheney White House relied more heavily than earlier occupants of the White House on the device of signing statements, declaring the administration's intention to enforce only particular provisions of a law. Therewith the president claimed for his office the de facto power of a line item veto and dealt preemptively with the issue of the constitutionality of some of the law's provisions, including provisions for congressional or judicial oversight, on the grounds that such provisions diminish the president's executive authority. Given the secretiveness of the president's office, signing statements were particularly vexing to those who held to the importance of checks and balances. Signing statements challenge the constitutional powers of Congress and the courts while denying to these bodies the information they need to mount a counterchallenge.

The presidential party also propounded a unitary executive theory, which further extended presidential power. This theory rejected the notion that other branches of government share some power with the executive branch, either through congressional oversight or through the existence of relatively autonomous agencies (independent of the president's power to hire and fire at will) that might issue reports and decisions not subject to the administration's editorial review. This strict top-down exercise of authority curtailed substantially the possibility of independent professional, scientific, legal, and professional judgments issuing out of the executive branch unfiltered by the president's political agenda.

The administration viewed its strengthening of executive power through the unitary executive theory as restoring rather than breaking with the past. President Bush himself looked to Theodore Roosevelt as his hero in the wielding of power. John Yoo, head of the Office of Legal Council in the Justice Department, and others cited the actions of Presidents Woodrow Wilson, Franklin D. Roosevelt, Truman, Lyndon Johnson, Nixon, and Reagan as showing the way toward a more powerful presidency.

Most importantly, the "presidentialists," as the team in the Justice Department and the vice president's office came to be called, held that the Constitution itself supports this unitary executive theory. Alexander Hamilton had argued in the *Federalist Papers* that the founders wisely vested executive leadership in a president, not in a committee and certainly not in a swarm of congressmen.[40] Unity is the indispensable precondition of strong, energetic leadership. Only a president can act with "decision, activity, secrecy, and dispatch" (no. 70). Yoo stretched out such "unity" at the head into a unitary power and command down the line with impermeable borders. While in the Office of Legal Counsel in the Justice Department he saw overlaps with the other branches of government as an inadmissible weakening of the president's power, especially in wartime.[41]

Critics of this unitary executive theory remind us that Hamilton was not the sole founding father of the country. The other great author of the *Federalist Papers*, James Madison, insisted on checks and balances in the exercise of power. The founders embedded checks and balances in the Constitution, and in the course of its ratification the country insisted upon a Bill of Rights because the nation might face the threat of tyranny not simply from abroad but from within.

Further, critics of unitary executive theory point out that Hamilton himself—in the very same paragraph in which he defended vesting executive power in a single hand, not in a committee—also insisted that a "numerous legislature" is "best adapted to deliberation and wisdom, and best calculated to conciliate the confidence of the people, and to pursue their privileges and interests" (*Federalist Papers*, no. 70). Yoo also ignored the balance in Hamilton's paragraph. Hamilton had carefully circumscribed the meaning of the president's role as commander in chief, as Yoo did not. Garry Wills noted that Hamilton defined the president as "commander in chief" in the sense of "first general of the army" (*Federalist Papers*, no. 69).[42] Hamilton did not refer to the president as the commander in chief of the United States. That title would have bestowed upon the president a kind of priority and preponderance of power in relation to the other branches of government, the public, and the Constitution itself that did not obtain then and should not obtain now.

LIMITING THE IMPERIAL SELF

A deep irony abounds in American history. Liberals, radicals, and conservatives—for different reasons in the last century—have inveighed against imperialistic and oppressive institutions. But they have not recognized that beneath imperialistic institutions often lies an equally imperial concept of the self. The need to placate the imperial self helps explain the air of unreality that haunted the Bush administration. After 9/11, the administration sounded the alarm for a world-historical struggle against terrorists and tyrants, yet it did not call for sacrifices from all Americans in the struggle. It rejected tax hikes to pay for the war; it dismissed the very idea of a draft, thus relying on those with the humblest of resources to fight it; and it advised the rest of the nation to go shopping. In another era W. H. Auden dealt with similar ironies in behavior when he warned of

the snarl of the abyss
That always lies just underneath
Our jolly picnic on the heath
Of the agreeable.[43]

In its policies the administration has scrupulously deferred to an imperial understanding of the self, calling for no serious limitations on the American way of life.

How may we define the imperial self so that it does not trivialize into some Napoleonic caricature? The literary critic Quentin Anderson, in his study of Ralph Waldo Emerson, Henry David Thoreau, and Walt Whitman, recognized the imperial self as the self that accepts no limitations upon itself at the hands of others.[44] It resents intrusions from the public realm. It does not invest itself in strong, nurturing, and self-restraining institutions. For the latter a society must cultivate the civic self.

The civic self, as opposed to the imperial self, understands and accepts itself as limited and amplified by others. Subjectively, the civic self has learned how to move out of the arena of purely private preference and to act, however imperfectly, in concert with others. Objectively, this work in concert with others must serve—at least in part—the common good. A society wholly driven by imperial self-interest would tear itself to pieces—no matter how ingenious its constitutional safety mechanisms of checks and balances—if it did not also cultivate the civic self. That is why the leaders of the revolutionary period (more than the immediately following constitutional period) recognized the importance of public virtue in a citizenry. "No phrase except 'liberty' was invoked more often by the revolutionaries than the 'public good.'"[45] Public virtue implies some readiness to sacrifice self-interest to the common good.[46]

Such sacrifices for the common good are important, both in the domain of politics and in the setting of what Burke called "the little platoons amongst us." Sociologists have dubbed the latter less elegantly "intermediate institutions"—neither the government nor the solitary individual—upon which the health and vigor of our common life depends. Such intermediate institutions include professional societies, neighborhood associations, religious congregations, and countless others. They have their own particular interests; but when they do their work well, they are not merely interest groups. They are also publics within the public at large, keeping at least one eye on the question of the common good. The discipline with which such publics act should serve as a brake both on the intemperate wants of the imperial self and on the ill-considered projects of an imperial government. At the same time, the habits of sacrifice they engender should help sustain those national policies that call for individual and group expenditures on behalf of just causes.

Religious communities, to the degree that they act as publics within the public at large and not merely as interest groups, are engaged in cultivating the civic self. They surely do not exist or meet for that sole purpose. But in the course of their common lives congregations learn something about the art of acting in concert with others for the common good. Rabbis, priests, and ministers lead groups of people of all stripes and purposes and cross-purposes. Their communities debate over commitments of time and money and reach decisions about priorities in common cause. And even though their leaders have done little to engage in what used to be called social action or in the cutting edge of a prophetic ministry, such leaders—in marrying and burying Democrats as well as Republicans, hawks as well as doves, and in drawing together people who may be recalcitrant and at odds—are engaged in building up indirectly the soil in which democratic institutions may flourish.

TAKING TO HEART MONOTHEISM
IN DEALING WITH DUALISTS

In this chapter I have not called the dualist movement—currently still forceful in our politics—the "Christian Right." Strictly speaking, its adherents, whether affiliated with a denomination or not, urge upon the country not Christianity but a different religion: dualism, not monotheism. Saint Augustine was the founding theologian in the West who recognized what is at stake here. In his great treatise on the dualism of his time he did not locate the Manichæan dualists on a spectrum of Christian left, center, and right, as though he were describing simply different colorations of the same thing.[47]

The metaphor of a spectrum of left, center, and right (which the modern media regularly imply when they refer to a Christian Right) assumes a single beam of light that refracts into different colors. Augustine recognized, on the contrary, that the dualists throw a different beam of light altogether, not simply an alternative shade of Christian monotheism. They are not a Christian Right. They are something different, and they are wrong.

Augustine made a second, even more important, point. He recognized the lure of dualism in us all. He himself had spent nine years as "a hearer" among the Manichees, attracted at first to the instant clarity they offered in the struggle of good and evil. He finally rejected dualism.

However, taking to heart his monotheism, Augustine also warned against adopting a dualistic view of dualists. He declared that "to heal heretics is better than to destroy them." God's will is "that they should be amended rather than destroyed. And in every case . . . we must believe that the designed effect is the healing of men, and not their ruin."[48]

Augustine recognized that if we want to address the destructive power of dualism at the deepest level, then we had better contain the lure of dualism in our own souls as we deal with them. That cautionary tale has reappeared in the testing events covered in this chapter. Israel needed a king to firm itself up against the threat of tyrants from without and to fend off anarchy from within. But it also needed to contain its own runaway fears so as not to install within its own life the arbitrary powers it feared.

The founders of the United States of America, having gone through thirteen years of ineffective national government, came to see the need for a stronger national executive and legislative authority to overcome the weakness of the former colonies in dealing with overseas tyrants and pirates on the high seas and rebellions from within. But they built a system of checks and balances into the Constitution, and they encouraged the cultivation of the civic self so as to bequeath a society more spaciously conceived than a nation obsessed with its security alone.

That imperfect republic, eventually grown powerful, has undergone two successive waves of anxiety since World War II, but it must not let an uncontained fear reconfigure it into shapes it professes to detest.

Most tellingly, however, Augustine's ideas offer a final warning to monotheists on the current scene. Monotheists will succumb to their own spiritual temptations if they simply slam the door shut on the dualists in their midst and create a reflexive dualism of their own—identifying the bad guys with any given set of threatening dualists and the good guys with the shifting band of monotheists in the churches. Believers in God as the Alpha and the Omega owe God a more hopeful, open, and confident politics than that, as they persist in working with all sorts and conditions of men and women—irregular libertarians and would-be imperialists, dualists and secularists, and religionists of every stripe—to build spacious, humane, and habitable institutions in the rough terrain of modern politics. A rough terrain, indeed, but whoever promised that pursuing the common good would be easy?

THE OVERREACH OF
FREE MARKET IDEOLOGY

Business and Government

The presidential election of 2004 troubled the nation more than most elections in living memory. The reaction went deeper than battles between Democrats and Republicans on particular issues. Policy differences reflected a far deeper struggle over identity—just who we are as a nation.

Politically the right attempted to redefine America. President George W. Bush's re-election, even though it was by a small majority of voters, tended to endorse this redefinition in the eyes of the world and to make it less reversible than his apparently accidental election by a five-to-four vote of the Supreme Court in 2000.

In foreign affairs this alteration in identity cast the nation in a role resembling that of imperial Rome. Whereas the founders of the country modeled America after Athens and republican Rome, the template under Bush bore an imperial stamp. A unilateralist foreign policy signaled a country that no longer perceived itself to be a republic but saw itself as the ruling power in a monopolar world.

Similarly, the country seemed engaged domestically in producing a two-class society that resembled the imperial city. As its first order of business, no matter what the circumstances, the Bush administration supported tax cuts for the wealthy and for corporate America: tax cuts before 9/11 and after 9/11; tax cuts before and after the invasion of Iraq; tax cuts during budget surpluses but also during budget deficits; tax cuts during America's huge shift from a manufacturing economy to a service economy and also during mounting trade deficits; and sadly enough, tax cuts for the wealthy, unaccompanied by other remedies, following the crash of 2008. Budget and trade deficits across the decade bankrolled consumer spending rather than investing in more competitive products and technologies. They also blocked those investments in infrastructure on which a robust future for a society depends.

Cumulatively, government policies helped create a permanent underclass—not the temporary underclass of newly arrived immigrants, but a permanent class of those who serve the highly placed but who do not adequately participate in the fundamental goods that a civilization offers.

The deterioration of neighborhoods in the inner cities, the decline of elemental safety—never mind education—in the public schools, the burgeoning of jail populations to the point that the country had the highest percentage of incarcerated citizens of any nation in the industrialized world, the great strains on the family, the general slackening of discipline that a consumer- and media-driven society relentlessly encourages, and the huge transfer of wealth in almost twenty-five years between 1977 and 1999 (during which the upper 1 percent of Americans more than doubled their share of all income and the lowest 20 percent suffered an actual decline)—all these changes signaled a civilization at risk.[1]

About 20 percent of American children lived in officially calculated (and therefore underestimated) poverty.[2] More than forty-five million Americans had no health care insurance; far more than twenty million were underinsured. About 80 percent of Americans without health care coverage were the working poor, whose children attended schools that were vastly overcrowded and underfunded, giving them little access to those skills that might help them negotiate life in an information age.

Social critics have worried about the eventual turmoil in store for a country that has created a *permanent* underclass or "internal proletariat." In his *Study of History* Arnold Toynbee defined an internal proletariat as a large body of people who are *in* a society but not *of* it, because they do not participate adequately in the society's benefits.[3] Measured by that standard, the wealthiest nation the world has ever seen has been industriously preparing the way for the fulfillment of Toynbee's prophecy that most "high civilizations" die not by the weapons of outsiders but eventually by their own hands. They die by suicide, not by murder.

That may well be. But the threat from the underclass does not yet pose the chief internal danger to good public order in the United States. In the late 1990s Barbara Ehrenreich spent some time in different locales in the East and Midwest working as a waitress, hotel maid, housecleaner, nursing home aid, and Walmart salesperson. She settled in the cheapest digs possible and tried to live on the $6.50 to $7.00 per hour one could expect at the time in such jobs. Even though the work itself was often mentally and physically exhausting, she discovered that she could not make it financially. In a cadenza at the end of her book *Nickel and Dimed*, this upperclass, professional writer concluded that the rest of us ought to feel shame—"shame at our dependency . . . on the underpaid labors of others." The "working poor," she observed, "are in fact the major philanthropists of our society. They neglect their own children so that the children of others will be cared for, they live in substandard housing so that other houses will be shining and perfect; they endure privation so that inflation will be low and stock prices high. To be a member of the working poor is to be an anonymous donor, a nameless benefactor, to everyone else."[4]

The term "philanthropist," of course, misleads as a description of the working poor. Benefactors give voluntarily, but underpaid workers often sacrifice under compulsion. They do not enjoy the freedom of movement that economic libertarians thoughtlessly impute to labor. Often lacking a car, the working poor cannot solve the problem of transportation or child care or special health needs, except by staying where they are. Because they are stuck in place, their sacrifices are many but are often compelled. Still, Ehrenreich has a point. The working poor have been remarkably generous in sustaining the social order.

The ruling class, not the poor, supplies the more worrisome symptoms of withdrawal from community. Historically, classical conservatives prized order and abhorred instability and chaos and therefore charged members of the ruling class with some duties toward others and the common good. In recent history too many of the powerful and wealthy have withdrawn from the responsibility of paying for war or for those fundamental goods on which a coherent civilization depends. Too many have engaged in what Robert Reich has called "the secession of the successful." They have tended, he says, to withdraw into gated communities with private security guards and "enclaves of good schools, excellent health care, and first rate infrastructures—all the while scoffing at almost all functions of government—thus cutting off the supply of taxes for most public undertakings—leaving much of the rest of the population behind."[5] Too many of the most powerful have abandoned the Puritan ideal of a "city built on a hill," language to which Ronald Reagan once appealed, and aspire instead to living like Romans—in a mansion behind walls.

INTO THIN AIR

In the first chapter's exploration of American foreign policy, two images help convey the dread of chaos: the images of fire and flood—the incineration of the twin towers and the engulfing events of Iraq and Katrina. Both images convey the destruction of durable forms. Recent experience on the domestic scene has exposed yet another symbol for the collapse of stable and weighty forms—the thin air into which they evanesce.

The disappearance of huge profits into the hands of the successful and the eventual bursting of the stock market and real estate bubbles in 2001 and 2007–8 saw the vanishing of apparently solid assets and successful institutions into the air, like gold dust scattering in the wind at the end of the movie *The Treasure of Sierra Madre*.

We witnessed, at the turn of the millennium, the sudden dissipation of institutions that seemed so tangibly ascendant—Enron, Worldcom, Global Crossing, McLeod USA, Cendant, Sunbeam, Waste Management, Dynegy, Qwest, Adelphia Communications, and Countrywide. Chief executives in these and many other firms had enjoyed salaries, bonuses, and other perks as much as 350 to 400 times the average salaries in their companies. The device of stock options kept actual corporate expenses against profits off the books, thus jacking up still further the value of stocks, either executive-owned or optable.[6] Some executives took advantage of insider knowledge to sell off their company stocks before the bubble burst, and most chief executives enjoyed golden parachutes to escape future financial contingencies of the sort that ordinary earthlings face.

The collapse of the real estate market in 2006–8 led reporter Roger Lowenstein to shift the imagery used to describe the financial catastrophe from "bubble" to "foam." Lenders extended to home buyers subprime mortgages that were insufficiently secured either by down payments or by stable salaries and that were often burdened in advance with huge balloon payments or upwardly adjusted rates. Meanwhile, the nonbank lender would often bundle as many as several thousand of these insubstantial mortgages into a security, misleadingly classified as an "asset-backed" security, and then petition (successfully) for a Moody triple-A bond rating.[7] The rating agencies (paid directly by the lenders seeking good ratings) too often served as well-paid alchemists rather than objective appraisers, and they converted B-grade dross into triple-A gold dust. Such securities, consisting of bundled mortgages, would then be assembled and serve as collateral in debt obligations (collateralized debt obligations, or CDOs, in the jargon of the trade) that might or might not hold their own in declining or even static markets.[8] Such derring-do worked under favorable market conditions when the original assets in real estate seemed salable and profitable. However, when overextended homeowners faced balloon payments and increased interest rates in 2007–8, such apparently grounded collateral floated off into thin air. For the second time in a decade another round of apparently durable great names, this time in banking and finance, either dissipated or gamed the system by betting on and profiting by its collapse.

In an increasingly global cyberspace economy, corporate leaders have tended to become an elusive, disembodied, aerial elite, emotionally protected by distance (and sometimes by telephone answering services in Bangladesh) from the mayhem and consternation their decisions have wrought. Kevin Phillips captured the pneumatic element in this withdrawal: Virtual corporations "were all head— for finance, legal, marketing, design, and research and development functions—and little or no body, in the sense of fixed marketing capacity."⁹ This picture of all head and no body conforms to our cartoon images of the ghostly, the apparitional.

Perhaps the most disembodied players in the modern economy have been hedge fund managers who amassed in a single year previously unimaginable fortunes. In 2007 the fifty richest managers earned a total of $29 billion, some of them profiting not from general prosperity but from the turmoil in the 2006–7 real estate market. Some operators anticipated and bet on the collapse of the real estate CDOs, making fortunes. Managers of private equity firms enjoy (unless reform is forthcoming) preferential tax treatment, paying only 15 percent of their earnings in taxes, whereas other people on salary or profits pay up to 35 percent. Operators can pass through their earnings at the lower rate as capital gains on investments, even though they are usually investing other people's money. Warren Buffett has wryly complained that the inequities in the tax system are so great that his secretary is taxed at a higher effective rate than he. More broadly, the inequities in wealth in the United States peaked to the point that, with one exception, one must reach back almost one hundred years to 1913 to match the contrast between the upper 1 percent who live above tree line and the populations in the valleys below.¹⁰

The implosion of the markets in September 2008 (a $6.9 trillion wipeout by the end of that year) led Thomas L. Friedman to offer a requiem on the latest round of boom, bubble, and bust. He observed that previous booms were damaging, but at least some of them left a tangible good in their wake. The nineteenth-century boom in railroad stocks left a railroad system spanning the continent; the prosperity after World War II produced an interstate highway grid; the late twentieth-century electronic boom left an Internet "highway" system in place. But the early twenty-first–century boom in the financial services industry would leave behind only "a bunch of empty Florida condos that never should have been built . . . private jets that the wealthy can no longer afford and dead derivative contracts that no one can understand. Worse, we borrowed the money from China, and now we have to pay it back with interest and without any lottery benefit."¹¹

The comments by Friedman, the congenital optimist, get at the meaning of a bubble. The "poof" at the end leaves nothing but thin air. Is it possible, however, that the bubble of 2007–8 leaves one unintended but important accomplishment within reach? Is there the possibility of a major political course correction in the United States? Might the country recognize the foolishness (and curb the political power) of the ideology that aspires to the gratification of all wants and that believes, against the evidence, that the mechanism of the marketplace if left to itself is self-corrective and needs no restraints? The country, as of 2010, has not offered a final answer to these questions.

THE FREE MARKET AGENDA

This chapter does not urge displacing the energy of the market place with a command economy. Instead, it explores and counters the dominant ideology since 1980 that has claimed for the marketplace itself an imperial authority that should operate largely unconstrained by other centers of power. So conceived, business is not merely one interest group among others; it rightfully wields a preeminent power over major aspects of the production and distribution of goods that some societies reserve to or share with the government and other institutions.

Business leaders wield a huge public power in the United States, which ideologues (and others only too readily) cloak and obscure by automatically calling it private enterprise. Corporate executives decide on industrial technology, patterns of organizing work, the locations of industries, market structures, the allocation of resources, and executive compensation and status. Their decisions produce momentous public impacts not only on investors but also on workers, neighbors, consumers, suppliers, and satellite service industries; on the air we breathe and the water we drink and bathe in; and on the forests and lakes to which we retreat on weekends.

The various resources on which business draws and the huge public impacts that it produces—on traffic patterns, school systems, parking accommodations, sewage plants, police and fire departments and other public facilities, and even on such fateful national decisions as going to war—constitute an extraordinary public power that cannot be defined as wholly private. Business leaders function as unelected public officials in a society like ours. Taking the long view of Western history, Charles E. Lindblom observed that two institutions—business and government—shape the modern world just as surely as the church and state molded the medieval world.[12]

Despite the great power of business today in all reaches of public life, some apologists for the free market would seek to knock down (or subordinate to market forces) all rival or constraining powers. They would seek to narrow the role of the government, co-opt the services of the professions, break the power of labor unions, marginalize (or mobilize) the churches, channel educational institutions largely to serve the market's needs for skilled technicians, and bankroll the media, through advertising, to fire up the appetites of a consumerist society and thus keep the business engine roaring. This chapter concentrates chiefly on the free market's agenda to narrow the permissible role of the government, the market's major competitor in the exercise of power.

Economic libertarians rank the government as the chief threat to business, but they do not oppose all government. They recognize the government's role in providing a stable framework for buying and selling in the marketplace and other voluntary exchanges. Thus they support taxes to provide security (fire, police, and defense departments), transportation (roads, bridges, highways, ports, and airports), and often, to a lesser degree, education.

However, they resist government efforts to address the unmet welfare needs of citizens for food, clothing, shelter, and health care and to support other common and high goods (such as a sustainable environment, high-quality public education, the arts, research, and common public spaces). In their vision the government overreaches its power and begins to constrict the liberty that legitimates its very existence if it uses its coercive power to tax for such purposes. It begins to resemble the robbers whom citizens funded in the first place to oppose.

Under the banner of "get the government off our backs," strict economic libertarians have opposed regulations that would ensure the safety of working conditions and products or that would protect the environment. They believe that the marketplace has its own built-in mechanisms that in the long run will punish opportunists and predators. Cheaters and exploiters will eventually lose business; their profits will dwindle. Economic libertarians would also dismantle government welfare programs that support jobs, housing, education, health care, and child care. Such Robin Hood activities, they complain, rob the hardworking and the well-to-do and corrupt the poor by establishing patterns of dependency.

Ultimately, they believe, the welfare state serves badly the economic interests of the poor. Redistributive taxes lead to a stagnant economy and fewer jobs, conditions from which the poor inevitably suffer. The government needs to get out of the way by reducing taxes and privatizing, as rapidly as possible, education, health care, and social security. Cutting taxes will unleash the productive power of the marketplace to create more wealth and plenty for all. Thus, the free market is not only self-correcting but transforming for the society fortunate enough to live within the arc of its power.

THE DEBATE

The vision of the basic autonomy of the market against the encroachments of the government rests on four arguments. First, management has a primary duty to stockholders to maximize profits. The verb "maximize" is inherently imperial. It tends to crowd out (or subordinate) all other interests, whether the stakes of workers, customers, neighbors, suppliers, or the public interest as expressed through the government. The latter interests figure only as contractual constraints in the course of fulfilling the stand-alone goal of maximizing profits for investors.

Apologists for the free market usually add to this argument based on duty a second, utilitarian appeal to the remarkable quantity, quality, and diversity of goods the market produces. (At the height of the Cold War, the East Berlin guards at Checkpoint Charlie used to confiscate as subversive materials, from pedestrians traveling from West into East Berlin, not only the Bible but that extraordinary proof of Western prodigality, the Sears-Roebuck catalog.) Further, the marketplace does not depend unduly on human virtue to produce its abundance of goods. That is its beauty, its magic. It begins with the ordinary dross of human motive—self-interest—and through the exchanges of buying and selling, multiplied thousands of times, it produces cumulatively the wealth of nations. The marketplace offers its prodigal public service through outcome rather than through purity of motive.

Apologists make a third argument that the modern free market emerged with democracy and offers the economic analogue and companion to it. Citizens legitimate the market by purchasing the goods that flow from its productivity. The voice of the people gets registered through the sale of products and through the job opportunities it offers. They vote according to their wants, and the market adjusts accordingly. Democratic government serves best as helpmate to the free markets when it remains small and deferential. Unfortunately, across two centuries taxes have increased in the United States from about 2 percent to 30 percent of the gross domestic product, pushing the original democracy, so the argument goes, toward the airless room of a command economy.

Finally, the free market is self-corrective in its operation. Government regulations are often stifling, slow-witted, and redundant. The law of supply and demand quickly corrects for changes in wants as signaled by unsold goods on the shelves. The mechanism also providentially punishes the indolent and imprudent who fail to work hard enough or wisely enough to serve their own self-interest; and it punishes opportunists and predators, because the latter eventually lose the trust on which their success with customers ultimately depends.

This conventional, prudential account of the self-corrective prowess of the marketplace expanded into the grander claim around 1970 that the stock markets operate with a near-perfect efficiency. Eugene Fama asserted in his influential 1970 article titled "Efficient Capital Markets" that the markets move with lightning speed so "that security prices at any given time 'fully reflect' all available information." The market regulates itself much more efficiently through its multiple transactions than a government clumsily does through taxes and regulatory statues. The government serves business best by deregulating—in effect by effacing itself.

Advocates of a mixed economy, among whom I number myself, counter the economic libertarians on each of the four arguments.

First, the imperial goal of maximizing profits for stockholders fails to honor other corporate duties to workers, customers, neighbors, and suppliers, who have varying but important stakes in corporate performance, sometimes deeper than those of stockholders. Investors often dart in and out of their investments (on the average at least once a year and usually more often). They move out of their stakes in a corporation more easily than do less mobile workers and neighbors who depend fatefully on its fortunes.

The public at large, through its taxes, has also invested deeply in sustaining both the general marketplace and particular corporations. Businesses profit handily from such public investments as road improvements, canals, railroads, airports, enclosure acts, stadiums, large tax credits for research (and the government's own research, from which private corporations handsomely benefit), huge tax offsets, the business rental of Defense Department plants at favorable rates, urban renewal projects to help retailers, special tax-free perquisites and fringe benefits for top management, and government investments to support the infrastructure of education and other services that enable business to recruit skilled workers. Having profited from these public resources and most recently from massive bailouts (to the tune of $700 billion from the Troubled Asset Relief Program [TARP] set aside in 2008), free marketers can hardly narrow corporate responsibility to the investments of stockholders alone.

The second argument, celebrating the efficiency (and creativity) of the market in producing commodities, deserves substantial but qualified support from advocates of a mixed economy. Economic libertarians carelessly neglect the costs and limitations of an unregulated market. They obscure the substantial social costs of productivity by dismissing as "externalities" damage to the environment, pollution (sometimes even injurious products and hazards within the workplace), jamming of the streets and schools, and shifts in business strategy that contribute to the decay of cities, small towns, and old suburbs.

Economic libertarians also tend to collapse the important distinction that a society needs to make between optional commodities and necessities. Access to optional commodities, like a tie and a scarf, can be left entirely to the vicissitudes of the marketplace. However, access to necessities like food, clothing, and shelter should not wholly depend on the vagaries of market distributions. Receiving a heart defibrillator should not ride entirely upon whether the patient surfaces on the radar screen of some provider as a profit opportunity.

Left to its own evaluations, a free market also tends to produce a society somewhat thin or tattered in its public resources. Such improvements as the quality of a nation's transportation and communication systems, its utilities, and its provision of clean air, water, soil, and energy all enable a society to serve its own continuance and the well-being of its citizens. We have come to rely on the dull-gray term "infrastructure" to describe these supportive public goods. Abraham Lincoln (and Daniel Webster and Alexander Hamilton before him) once termed them "internal improvements." A modern architect might liken infrastructure to the basic bones of a building upon which all its inhabitants depend.

In response to the economic libertarians' third argument, it must be conceded that modern democracy has emerged with the rise of the free markets; but democracy serves neither the markets nor itself well simply as an echo chamber. Democracy needs the distinctive voice of the voting booth, the courts, and the legislative halls to protect citizens from some of the damage and self-damage wrought by an unregulated market and to compensate for the market's limitations in meeting societal needs.

The conservative link of democracy with a small, deferential government misreads American history. Admittedly, the government collected little from direct taxes on citizens in its early decades. Nevertheless, the government could advance national purposes in other ways. Relatively invisible, indirect taxes on imports helped; and as the nation's largest landowner, the government hugely influenced the country's growth through the support of railroads, public schools, forestry, mines, canals, and road building. Further, the government countered some of the economic inequalities of an expanding industrial society by the sale and lease of land for small farming. The chief resource that enabled the government to do such work shifted from land to taxes toward the end of the nineteenth century, as the need for government interventions increased.[13] Today, only the government can match the corporation and the markets as a countervailing and supplementary power.

The final argument, citing the self-corrective prowess of the marketplace, has lost ground in recent decades. Some of the market's corrections come at a huge social cost. Its often fateful, distant operations can cruelly devastate the hardworking but vulnerable.

The too-frequent infestation by cheats, frauds, and exploiters of un-enforced or nonexistent regulations (from Enron to Bernie Madoff in recent years) confounds the claim that the market effectively punishes its scoundrels. More than three million corporations operate worldwide with no identifiable owners, and wealthy individuals may control as much as $17 trillion in assets in jurisdictions with opaque and bank secrecy laws. Offshore tax havens have cost the United States $350 billion in lost revenue.[14]

The crash of 2008 posed a still deeper challenge to the claim that the market is self-corrective. The crash exposed the inability of the market not simply to correct the moral failure of some of its members but to correct itself systemically. Wall Street and Main Street suffered a seizing up of the entire system of lending and borrowing, buying and selling. The crash resembled the multiple systems failure sometimes suffered by the elderly when the pulmonary system shuts down or the nervous system sputters, fearful and distrustful. The shutdown spreads rapidly from system to system. As Michael Lewis put it, "When banking stops, credit stops, and when credit stops, trade stops, and when trade stops—well, the city of Chicago had only eight days of chlorine on hand for its water supply. Hospitals run out of medicine. The entire modern world was premised on the ability to buy now and pay later."[15]

In response to the crash the momentarily dwindling band of libertarian purists resisted crisis interventions. Let faltering companies fail, they grimly affirmed. Only by such failures will the market purge itself and carry on. However, in the face of systemic collapse, other members of the corporate community jettisoned the doctrine of the market as self-corrective. Merrill Lynch, Bear Sterns, Lehman Brothers, Fannie Mae and Freddie Mac, AIG, and at length General Motors and Chrysler sought government bailouts, loans, infusions of cash, or backups when they faced financial straits. They wanted to be spared the dark side of the "creative destruction" that capitalism inspired and that almost all had once proudly celebrated—in the abstract.

A second, less libertarian, response to the 2008 breakdown emerged under the aegis of the Bush administration. Bush explained that we are libertarian in ordinary times and interventionist only in extraordinary times. That sharp distinction blurs a difficulty.

Unregulated liberty and low taxes in ordinary times create a momentum that leaves a government weakened in resources to intervene in extraordinary times. Further, what guides the need for a specific intervention in extraordinary times? The high-powered Bush team of Secretary of the Treasury Henry Paulson, Chair of the Federal Reserve Ben Bernanke, and Timothy Geithner, then head of the Federal Reserve in New York, candidly admitted that in "unprecedented circumstances" they were making up their decisions on rescue funds as they went along. In due course they justified an intervention if a specific breakdown threatened to push the whole system over the cliff. AIG got money; Lehman Brothers did not. That working principle quickly led wags to suggest that if you are big enough, you get money. If the country would go down when you go down, help is on the way.

Eventually, the Bush team called in leaders of the nine great houses of finance, all facing some degree of trouble either directly or indirectly, and pressured them to accept billions of dollars to establish a fire wall against the flaming-out of the entire fiscal system. Unfortunately, the government made available the greater portion of the first $350 billion of rescue funds without adequate assurance that the recipients of the money would act to help the system recover from its seized state. Institutions that had increased their risks without limit in the manic phase of the real estate bubble now sat tight on their money while still paying out their customary, unseemly bonuses to their partners and top traders. Almost no help trickled down to the 10 percent of American homeowners who faced bankruptcy or to the growing numbers of the jobless or to struggling merchants on Main Street. An overheated system was swinging into its opposite—cold, fearful, and miserly. Millions of bit players—workers, the jobless, merchants, and consumers—shut down accordingly.

THE KEYNESIAN ALTERNATIVE

In its wild swings an unregulated economy seems to ride successively the two horses of love and fear: the love of money and the fear of its loss. The great interpreter of the severe market swings of the 1920s and 1930s, John Maynard Keynes, apparently saw the second swing as a subset of the first. In an unpublished paper (1925), he identified two kinds of love of money: (1) "the objectless pursuit of wealth" and (2) "the disposition to 'hoard,' or not spend money."[16] (Echoes of the theological tradition, to which Keynes himself did not subscribe, appear in Keynes's recognition that "the love of money is the root of all evil" [1 Tm 6:18]. See chapter 4 in this book for an attempt to show why Augustine has a deeper hold on the dynamics of objectless desire than does Keynes in his account of money as abstract.)

The first kind of love of money is objectless and abstract in that it does not seek to rest satisfied in particular goods it purchases. Money has the spectral advantage of always enticing the pursuer to press forward beyond what he or she has and to take risks in order to acquire yet more. Such risk taking is not lazy and blind. The pursuer engages in due diligence and uses mathematical models today to hone skills in risk management. So honed, these skills in risk taking in the pursuit of still greater wealth supply the engine of capitalism.

The second form of the love of money outlined by Keynes—the disposition to hoard—reflects the psychology of the miser. The miser's disposition acts as a brake on capitalism because it abhors risk taking. Still, risk takers and hoarders resemble one another in that they share a "disposition to value money above the things it could buy. This disposition is true of both the moneylender and the money hoarder."[17] Keynes's biographer, Robert Skidelsky, also sees hoarding basically as a subset of the love of money. That placement seems wrong. By locating hoarders in the economic context of uncertainty, a state of being beyond the radius of ordinary risk taking, Keynes and Skidelsky seem to place hoarders psychologically in the matrix of anxiety and fear, not love.

In any event, a free market economy tends to chafe at the intrusions of government. In the market's manic phase free marketeers resist government regulations, investments, and taxes as constrictions on the ability of players in the market to engage without limit in the pursuit of still more money. In the market's contracting phases, hoarders retreat to the security that money supplies in the midst of surrounding uncertainty. They recoil from inflationary borrowing, stimulating, investing, and taxing on the part of government that would seem to deplete their resources.

Keynes proposed a political remedy of countercyclical fiscal policies: the government should tax and regulate in good times and spend in bad times. This remedy runs counter to the prevailing dispositions of free marketeers in good times and bad. Free marketeers see the key problem in both phases as that of production. Lowering taxes, especially on the wealthy, helps create the savings to be invested in production, which will eventually trickle down to produce jobs. So goes the theory of supply-side economics. Keynes and his followers believed, to the contrary, that in a society like ours the key problem is not production but consumption, not supply but demand. More than any other factors, unemployment and great inequalities in wealth will stall an economy because they dry up market demand. Thus, the market needs taxes in good times (income, inheritance, and excise taxes) to sustain a broad market demand. The wealthy will survive somewhat higher taxes. The existence of a strong market demand, much more than lower taxes, will inspire the wealthy to invest in production and thereby create new jobs.[18] By the same token a down market needs government to borrow and invest and spend prudently—not in order to demolish the marketplace, but to invigorate, stabilize, and rescue it from its excesses and its abstractions from human good.

The reader may recognize here a resemblance between Kennan's emphasis on the importance of America's self-containment in foreign policy and Keynes's recommended discipline in economic policy, summarized in the phrase "countercyclical fiscal policies." Through such policies a government would help counter in the marketplace the dangerous swings in appetites and fears.

GOVERNMENT INTERVENTIONS: TO RESCUE, REGULATE, STIMULATE, AND REDIRECT

President Barack Obama's economic team included, among others, Federal Reserve chair Bernanke and Geithner, subsequently the secretary of the treasury. They continued President Bush's code-blue effort to rescue and resuscitate the fiscal system but insisted on greater transparency, oversight, and accountability in the expenditure of the last half of the $700 billion TARP rescue package; not an easy task. The country needed a more transparent, accountable doctor. But the doctor, in this case the government, had to deal with a patient whose lab values were opaque. Just how profoundly compromised were particular banks or investment houses in the complicated mix of off-balance sheet operations, auction-rate securities, insurance credit swaps, securities based on bundles of subprime mortgages, leveraged buyouts, and sundry innovative products? Were many of these claimed assets toxic or necrotic? Would a taxpayer rescue operation in the midst of excessive bonuses (newly named "retention awards") simply underwrite an economy that socialized loss and privatized profit? Meanwhile, the effort to rescue Wall Street did not trickle down to Main Street and jobs. Popular reactions to the government intervention tended to overlook its great accomplishments: It saved the financial system from what could have ended in its total collapse, and most of the banks eventually repaid their direct loans from the government, though not their larger indebtedness for being spared a total collapse.

THE EFFORT TO REGULATE

From the end of 2008 toward the middle of 2009, the government concentrated on rescuing the economic system from its free fall. It deferred until later—at considerable political cost to itself—developing a package of federal regulations to prevent an unacceptable repeat of earlier out-of-control cycles. Legislators in the US House and Senate hoped to complete the final bill by the summer of 2010. It would protect consumers (on car loans, mortgages, credit cards, and payday loans), perhaps shareholders (on the composition of corporate boards and on runaway executive compensation), and investors (by changes in the funding of credit rating agencies). The government would strengthen continuing oversight by updating and enforcing rules that govern commercial banks, by expanding regulations to cover investment houses and hedge funds, and by exposing to the light the "shadow banking system" that has developed in the United States. It would also require complex products such as derivatives to be insured and exchanged in the light of day, and it would rein in banks' proprietary investments that do not benefit their clients. Finally, it would curb fiscal maneuvers by which commercial and investment banks leverage themselves into a kind of bogus

immortality—too big to fail and thus beyond the reach of bankruptcy. When an institution needs dismantling, a procedure would
also be in place to avoid chaos but not allow the company to survive.
Its "resolution" should resemble "hospice, not convalescence."[19]
Those were basic intentions as of June 2010.

SAPPING REGULATORY POWER THROUGH LOW TAXES

The federal power to regulate, along with its other activities, depends heavily on the power to tax. "Starving the beast" of government through low taxes enfeebles the funding of regulatory agencies
that have bearing on the financial and other industries. Low funding for regulatory agencies, including the Internal Revenue Service
(IRS), also compromises the IRS's ability to collect those taxes
already on the books. From 1989 to 1999, the IRS suffered a 26
percent decrease in permanent employees, despite a 14 percent increase in tax returns to monitor. Prosecutions of tax cheats dropped
by half from what they had been ten years earlier; and the government selectively audited citizens making less than $200,000 a year
much more often than they audited the wealthy, partly because the
tax-avoidance measures followed by the wealthy are especially difficult to monitor and enforce.[20] Although the cascade of corporate
scandals in 2002 led to an expansion of the regulatory functions and
personnel of the Securities and Exchange Commission (SEC),
within three months after the bill's passage in July 2002 the administration cut back additional funding for the SEC by 27 percent.
Such funding maneuvers simultaneously undercut the power of the
government to regulate while they feed contempt for the government's inability to do its job. The enemies of government thus enjoy
a double win. The government's ineffectualness justifies still further
cuts in the tax rate. That double win broadens out to weaken yet a
further range of regulatory agencies that bear on worker safety, toxic
products, dangerous emissions that hasten global warming, and
lethal extractions of carbons from earth and water. The spring of
2010 alone saw a major mine disaster in West Virginia and the catastrophic hemorrhaging of oil in the Gulf of Mexico from a drill
hole some five thousand feet below the surface. Oil had poisoned
an area the size of the state of South Carolina before the well was
shut in July and cemented in August, but scientists disagree on how
far the oil plume has spread and at what rate.

THE CORRUPTION OF REGULATORS

Clearly, regulations can fail not simply because of insufficient funding but because of the incompetence and corruption of regulators. At the country's founding Madison justified the device of checks and balances to help ensure that the government itself would be checked in its governing. The country has needed not only the good offices of that device but also the cultivation of citizens devoted to the ideal of public service. In turn, both the device of checks and balances and the ideal of public service require that regulators demand accountability and transparency not only of corporate giants but of themselves. Otherwise, regulation slackens into lax monitoring and, worse yet, crony capitalism.

Despite their public avowals, some business and political leaders have long resembled crony capitalists more than libertarians. Their agenda has not been "get the government off our backs" but "get on the back of the government and direct it." The politician's need for campaign money greases the way in the United States for the domination of government by powerful special interests. Lobbyists and bundlers of campaign funds help keep politicians in office and reward some pliant politicians and administrators with a soft landing in good jobs when they leave government service. Usually nothing so gross as a quid pro quo arrangement transpires. A general disposition to provide business with a favorable climate slides into preferential treatment and weakens efforts to regulate evenhandedly or at all.

EFFORTS TO STIMULATE AND REDIRECT

The Obama team of Bernanke and Geithner recognized that the market system needed further measures both to stimulate the economy and to reform and redirect its priorities so that the patient did not return to the streets, its bad habits ominously still in place. The next $800 billion would need to stimulate the economy partly through tax incentives; partly by helping strapped state governments meet the health, welfare, and educational needs of stricken citizens; and partly through "shovel-ready" government projects. Keynesian economists such as Paul Krugman felt that the original rescue package and the following stimulus package were not enough and that the government routed the packages too obsequiously through Wall Street to stimulate the economy at large.

While breathing life into the broader economy, the government also needed to redirect the economy toward long-neglected goals that would serve the nation's fitness: investments in health care, public education, mass transportation, and the development of less toxic and more sustainable energy sources. Some such investments were twofers or even "threefers," in that they would not only serve the nation's general welfare but also help create jobs and sustain the nation's long-term competitiveness and security.

Some conservative Republicans favored, in the exceptional crisis of 2008, the rescue of the fiscal system and seemed favorably disposed to some regulations of the banks, but they opposed stimulating the economy (other than through tax cuts) and restructuring priorities for the long-range future. Big government, they assumed, will diminish the marketplace and silence democracy. Obama's proposals will land us in an alien European socialism, warned Newt Gingrich, the former speaker of the House of Representatives and now a conservative author and commentator.

A more subtle line of criticism came from David Brooks, columnist for the *New York Times* and a frequent voice on Jim Lehrer's *PBS NewsHour.* He and others argued that Obama should concentrate on the rescue effort alone. He should not try to do too much. Senator Lamar Alexander (R-TN) appealed to the example (somewhat off the mark) of President Dwight Eisenhower's clarion promise, "I shall go to Korea." Obama should concentrate on the fiscal rescue plan as his sole priority. Other matters could wait. (One guesses that some advisors in the White House also felt that for political reasons other matters, like health care reform, could wait.)

President Obama argued otherwise and invoked another president, Abraham Lincoln, in his basic response. No president has faced a more consuming task than Lincoln did in holding together the Union during the Civil War. Nevertheless, Lincoln undertook some major long-term internal improvements that the country needed: a continental railroad system, the Morrill Act establishing land grant colleges, and the Homestead Act.

Similarly, at a time of crisis Obama believed he needed to address problems, too long deferred, that in fact overlap with the fiscal and economic plight of the country. The government could not conveniently separate what it does in the emergency room to rescue the fiscal system from what it must begin to do on the issues of energy, education, and health care. The problems interconnect. Further, the president, like all presidents, needed to act while he still had wind at his back. The year 2009 seemed to be a teachable moment in American life. However, teachable moments in politics quickly pass. Obama suffered a decline in his political capital following each controversial decision along the way, and he would soon face swerving events such as the magnitude of the Gulf oil disaster in 2010, suggesting in the fall election of 2010 that this teaching moment had passed.

The political cost of rescuing the fiscal system was particularly high given the legitimate populist rage over the unconscionable $165 million in bonuses paid out to 418 employees by the conglomerate AIG, a recipient so far of nearly $200 billion in public monies. (Some fifty-two employees, receiving more than $33 million in bonuses, soon left the company—so much for a retention strategy. A total of seventy-three employees in AIG's financial products division—the unit that produced the company's near collapse and helped trigger the global financial crisis—received $1 million each.[21] So much for targeting the best and the brightest.) As of this writing, the administration, now 80 percent owner of AIG, hesitates to break contracts or punitively (and probably unconstitutionally) tax current or former employees. The government would lose credibility in doing business and suffer increases in its costs of borrowing just when the government needs money to rescue a seized-up economy and the country is massively indebted to China and other nations. Shades of Hamilton! Despite withering populist reactions, Hamilton backed a federal policy of absorbing past war debts and near worthless bank scrips held by speculators to shore up the future creditworthiness of the young nation.[22]

Political leaders cannot expect much gratitude for the costly repair of a problem largely (but not entirely) of someone else's making. Even beneficiaries of the current fiscal rescue quickly cite the cost of that rescue as a reason why the government cannot afford to do anything further to mend the education system or develop alternative sources of energy. They recall that such reforms take money, and money means taxes.

At this writing in 2010, the government is the only power left standing (by virtue of its capacity to borrow, lend, and above all, tax) with sufficient resources to rescue, stimulate, and redirect the clogged energies of a market economy. Six years before he assumed the office of president, Lincoln scribbled notes on the role of government: "The legitimate object of government is to do for people what needs to be done, but which they cannot, by individual effort, do at all, or do so well by themselves." Lincoln then divided the ends of government into two objects, negative and positive: those ends that follow "from the injustice of men," such as "all crimes, misdemeanors, and non-performance of contracts" and war; and those ends that require combined action, such as "making and maintaining roads, bridges, providing for the helpless, young, and afflicted, and schools."[23] Later, of course, the second and more positive role of government would be honored by the Lincoln administration with the building of the transcontinental railroad, the Homestead Act, and the Morrill Act.

On February 12, 2009, the two-hundredth anniversary of Lincoln's birth, Obama—a speaker with considerable reason to choose his words carefully—reminded his audience of Lincoln's call for the positive role of government articulated some 154 years before:

> Our current problems result . . . from a failure to meet the test that Lincoln set. . . . For we now know that tax cuts cannot provide much-needed relief to working families, tax cuts alone cannot rebuild our levees or our roads or our bridges. They cannot refurbish our schools or modernize our health care system. By themselves, they cannot lead to the next scientific breakthrough or great medical discovery or yield research and technology that will spark a clean energy economy. Only a nation can do these things. Only by coming together, all of us, and expressing that sense of shared sacrifice and responsibility—for ourselves and one another—can we do the work that must be done in this country.[24]

Voluntary communities may contribute substantially to a society's sense of shared sacrifice and responsibility, but sooner or later the willingness of the people in a democratic society to be taxed and taxed fairly tests their readiness to pay for what needs to be done. So Oliver Wendell Holmes Jr. reminded his fellow citizens in a sentence now paraphrased and chiseled above the entryway to the IRS building in Washington, DC: "I like to pay taxes. With them, I buy civilization."[25]

3

FREE MARKET IDEOLOGY

Bearing on Other Centers of Power

Critics of free market ideology concentrate chiefly on the contest in power between business and government. However, other centers of power have a public responsibility, independent of their relations to either the marketplace or the government. This chapter focuses primarily on the relations of the marketplace to these other institutions—the professions, unions, universities, the churches, and the media—as the market bears heavily on their operations.[1]

CO-OPTING THE PROFESSIONS

The professions of law and accounting provide the chief interface of business with the government and the public. The two professions purportedly guard the common good. Accountants belong to the only profession that explicitly carries the word "public" in its self-description—that is, "certified public accountant." The word "accountant" implies a means of securing corporate accountability to the public. But accountants compromise the clarity and integrity of their public role when they define themselves as makeup artists, accenting quarterly reports for the sake of boosting stock market prices or distorting annual returns to avoid tax exposure.

The Enron Corporation relied on the ingenuity of its accountants to give the illusion of glowing financial health. Accountants obligingly treated as profits in hand the merely anticipated long-range sales of assets acquired on borrowed money. This sleight-of-hand obscured the large number of variables that put such favorable outcomes beyond Enron's reach. The lure of profits also produced a kind of mission creep in the practice of accounting, which the great firms sold to their clients under the catchy title of "one-stop shopping centers." Some of the "big six" (so numbered at the time) accounting firms offered not only accounting and auditing but also consulting services to their clients. Some accountants (and lawyers) even entered into partnerships with their clients by devising entities that yielded themselves a percentage of ownership in an undertaking. Fire walls were built to protect the probity of the original accounting and auditing functions, but conflicts of interest became hard to contain. The financial yields from add-on enterprises overwhelmed the ordinary compensation for professional services, thereby affecting the balance between competing cultures within the accounting firm. Service to the common good tended to melt away.

Traditionally, lawyers have considered themselves among the professions obliged to guard the common good. Roscoe Pound, the great jurist, famously wrote that the term "profession" "refers to a group . . . pursuing a learned art as a common calling in the spirit of public service—no less a public service because it may incidentally be a means of livelihood."[2] Lawyers purportedly must serve their clients under the constraints of their status and duties as officers of the courts. However, in the adversary system the particular service of defense attorneys as court officers lies in their loyalty to their clients, who in a democracy enjoy legal protection, even when they are in dispute with their fellows or at odds with the laws of the state. Thus the professional, for the sake of the common good, does not act directly as an agent of the state. In protecting under the law the rights of the lawbreaker, the deviant, and the distressed, the professional also serves society. The lawyer serves as an officer of the court even when defending the client against the state's prosecution.

Well and good. However, an imbalance sets in. Apologists for the zealous defense attorney in the adversary system usually invoke the picture of the powerless, resourceless individual pitted against the majesty of the state. But given the distributions of money and talent in the marketplace, the gifted lawyer today more often than not works for a large corporation. The poor and the middle classes often cannot pursue their grievances in court. Inequities in the distribution of legal talent and delaying tactics in the courtroom often stack the deck in favor of the powerful.

The adversarial system, moreover, can encourage antinomianism in the client. The expert lawyer lets the client know how much he or she can maximally get away with. The lawyer treats the law not as a minimal statement of obligations to the neighbor that points beyond itself to a higher righteousness, but rather as a bright line that aids and abets the client's attempt to crowd the border of unrighteousness. Client advocacy surely is the attorney's public duty. But even duties to the client often require something more than an aggressive full-court press up to the limits of the law. Abraham Lincoln put it succinctly: In pushing to the limit of the law, the nominal winner may well be the real loser. In addition to serving as advocate *for* the client the lawyer may also need to be advocate *to* the client. Otherwise, the lawyer treats the client as merely a bundle of declared interests that the lawyer is hired to serve, not as a moral being susceptible to the just claims of others.

Following the scandals at the beginning of the twenty-first century, the Senate Judiciary Committee searched for legislative remedies that would stiffen the backbone of accountants and lawyers against the imperial overreach of large corporations such as Enron. Susan P. Koniac, testifying before the committee, reminded the body, "Twelve years ago in a court opinion dealing with some aspects of the Lincoln Savings and Loan Fraud, Judge Stanley Sporken wrote: 'Where . . . were . . . the accountants and attorneys . . . ? . . . With all the professional talent involved (both accounting and legal), why [did not] at least one professional [act] to stop the overreaching that took place in that case?'" "Now," said Koniac, "There is Enron. And we are here asking the same questions Judge Sporkin and others were asking twelve years ago."[3]

Legislation, such as the Sarbanes-Oxley Act, followed the Senate inquiry. The act holds professionals accountable for specific steps in response to their clients' behavior. Some professionals chafe at accepting that moral and legal burden; others smile at the prospect of shouldering it because the reform simply supplies professionals with more paid work to do. Both responses remind us that, to be effective, legislation and codes of conduct need active support from the ethos within the guilds themselves.

Lawyers operating with integrity in the adversary system cannot simply punt the question of achieving just outcomes to the decisions of judges. As officers of the court they should serve as advocates to their clients, not simply for them. Their independence as lawyers calls for the classical virtues of temperance and courage in dealing with their clients. These virtues are not easily come by. Fiercely competing in the marketplace today, law firms have normalized and encouraged runaway desire, as they extravagantly compensate their rainmakers and distribute monies on the principle of "eat what you kill." Moreover, runaway desire quickly generates runaway fears and worries that may control the lawyer's tongue. The avaricious lawyer serves the client with a slippery cunning; the fearful lawyer holds his or her tongue before abusive displays of power. In hanging on to their clients, lawyers are tempted to suppress words and deeds that might offend. In serving the common good, lawyers need not only guild and legislative standards but the courage to refuse being co-opted while earning their livelihood.

BREAKING THE POWER OF THE UNIONS

From the mid-1930s until the 1970s the union movement exerted substantial power in American life, despite the Taft-Hartley Labor Management Relations Act of 1947, which significantly limited labor's organizing power. The percentage of American workers in unions more than doubled, from 12 percent in 1935 to 27 percent in 1970. In addition to wielding negotiating power in particular industries, unions also organized the labor vote in elections. Their very existence often prompted managers in nonunionized industries defensively to grant their workers higher wages and benefits. The negotiating power of unions also kept top management from pushing their own compensation packages into orbit. From 1940 to 1975 the United States experienced greater income equality than it did in the gilded ages either preceding or succeeding it. Up to the crash of 2008 the income of those in top management averaged 350 to 400 times that of average workers in the firms they managed, as opposed to the ratio of 15 to 20 times that obtained during the more egalitarian period from 1940 to 1975.

The prevailing analysis of the current extreme income disparity attributes it to a variety of economic factors. The power of unions to negotiate (and governments to tax) has inevitably diminished, as corporations have faced the headwinds of global competition. Under pressure, executives have simply moved their operations overseas. The protracted US shift from an industrial economy (in which unions flourished) to an information age and a service economy has led to higher rewards for better educated managers and lower pay for unskilled and unorganized service workers. America has shifted economically from the hitherto ascendant General Motors to the union-shy Walmart.

However, critics have disagreed with the economic determinism of this analysis. They point out that both European and Eastern Rim nations compete today under roughly the same conditions as the United States but have not departed from the more egalitarian patterns of compensation that once prevailed in America. Paul Krugman argued that the dominant political ideology (from the years of Ronald Reagan forward) in the United States, not economic factors alone, has created the current gap between the rich and the working poor in the United States. Political ideology has pushed us into huge inequalities. By implication, a better politics can extricate us from them.[4]

Neoconservative apologists such as William Kristol (writing before the recession of 2008) have countered that income inequalities have irritated leftists but not ordinary people. The successes of the rich have not lessened a sense of equality among Americans or yielded a divisiveness in the nation. The nation divides over social and cultural issues—abortion, same-sex marriage, and the like—but not over the wealth of someone like T. Boone Pickens. Far better to emulate the Texas tycoon than to raise his taxes.

Kristol's brand of egalitarianism now seems abstract and distant, a hard sell to workers who have lost their jobs and see the ability to feed, clothe, shelter, educate, and supply health care for their families slipping beyond their reach. The gilded age of the last thirty years has been particularly hostile to the embodied needs of workers. Under the banner of "lean and mean," boards of directors promised lavish bonus and stock options to managers who increased profits by cutting costs. Firing workers often gave top managers the quickest route to the profits that hiked their own salaries and the value of their stock options. Within the corporation solidarity and loyalty were shattered for victims, survivors, and executioners alike. The directors gave large rewards to managers who earned their pay by ordering shipmates to walk the plank, while the messy human consequences of this decimation lay hidden in the antiseptic term "reengineering."

A particularly worrisome second strategy of "lean and mean" emerged. Some (not all) devotees of downsizing personnel and benefits insisted on downsizing government, also. They denied to the government the taxes that would enable it either to hire unemployed workers for projects that would improve the nation's infrastructure (the country still enjoys the benefits of projects undertaken by the Works Progress Administration [WPA] and the Civilian Conservation Corps [CCC] in the 1930s) or to provide supplements to the working poor who cannot meet basic needs from their low wages. In effect, some leaders wanted to have it both ways. For the sake of profits they denied their responsibility for providing continued employment and benefits to workers, and in order to reduce taxes on those profits they would deny to the government, even as a last resort, the power to ensure that citizens can survive and participate in the economic life of the nation.

If political ideology has created the problem, can an activist politics lead to the remedy? Krugman argued so in *Conscience of a Liberal*. He said that removing some of the barriers to organizing labor unions would help redress the income disparities in the country. The Democrats devised and introduced, unsuccessfully, an Employee Free Choice Act in the 111th Congress in 2008 with that purpose in mind. Reinvigorated unions might improve workers' wages and benefits and support government regulations to protect worker health and safety. The often industry-specific agenda of a union hardly guarantees support for and sometimes conflicts with other societal goals, such as environmental protection, a community-based health care system, and improvements in the quality of public education.

The unusual presidential campaign of 2008 highlighted another possible future political strategy for the Democrats not tied to the strength of the unions. A populist politics emerged in 2008 that depended less on union organizers and representatives and more on e-mail and text messaging. While technology helped weaken the labor movement by eliminating jobs and sending them overseas, it may also have created the blogging and e-mailing platforms by which huge numbers of people can connect and interact and mobilize resources and counter dominant power.

Reagan, a populist, emerged as a public figure on television with the early sponsorship of corporate power: General Electric. Barack Obama, a populist with a different message, emerged as a public figure on television with the help of text messaging.

Will Obama produce major political change? Simply electing him (along with a working Democratic majority in Congress) in 2008 did not dispose of the question. It has yet to be decided whether an indeterminately congregated mass of supporters can sustain specific legislative remedies for particular problems. New legislation inevitably entails a coefficient of adversity in the form of taxes and changes in habits and new demands that fall unequally on different people and on differently organized (or yet to be organized) interest groups. Enduring change depends on more than the charismatic gifts of a particular person; it also needs more embodied and vertebrate structures in place, such as the professions, unions, and various corporate and third-sector institutions, to weather the storms.

CHANNELING THE UNIVERSITIES

The professional guild has invoked the principle of academic freedom to resist the direct control of the classroom by donors, alumni, the government, and corporations. By and large, faculty members do not simply channel the voices of their patrons in the legislative halls and the board rooms of the nation. But the twentieth-century positivist university massively redefined the public aims and intentions of a university education and pointed its resources and personnel toward preparing students for their important roles in the marketplace.

Historically, the liberal arts provided young people with a privileged respite from pursuit of a society's marketplace needs and let students and the country consider afresh its fundamental aims and goals. The liberal arts differed self-consciously from the purely servile arts, the sole purpose of which was to supply young people with the skills to pursue artfully society's already established goals. The liberal arts sought to cultivate critical intelligence, as distinguished from operational intelligence. Operational intelligence helps one get from here to there, whereas critical intelligence poses the question as to whether the "there" is worth getting to. It asks what has been recently and thuddingly called the question of values.

The professional schools need to train for skills, but they also need to sharpen critical intelligence to reflect on questions of ends and values. Behind many of the quandaries of medicine—whether to pull the plug, whether to tell the truth—loom critical questions about the basic goal of medicine. Is it an unconditional fight against death? Or the elimination of suffering? Or the pursuit of health? What basic values justify the legal system? The quest for truth and justice, or the sometimes opposing value of order? On these questions turn the justification and the potential reform of the adversary system. What purpose defines the goal of the corporation? Maximizing profit? Or the somewhat more complicated notion of economic performance at a profit? What defines the common good for the political leader? The overlapping interests of a coalition of interest groups? Something more?

To the degree that the university ignores these questions, it threatens the professions with their moral impoverishment, as they turn out technicians incapable of or hostile to critical thinking; and it also diminishes itself by stunting its intellectual life. The university is precisely the site where critical inquiry should dig into the deep places where a civilization hurts and explore alternative goals for the society at large and the professions in particular. We concede too little to the range of the human mind and grant too little to the capacity of the university to organize itself for civil and fruitful discourse if we limit its contribution to the servile arts. Critical inquiry is not only licit but required in the institution devoted to cultivating the whole of the human mind.

RELIGIOUS COMMUNITIES: MARGINALIZED (OR MOBILIZED)

Like critical inquiry in the academy, the prophetic, critical voice of the mainline Protestant churches has become muted on domestic political issues during the last fifty years. One episode highlights an important part of the problem economically. In the mid-1950s young faculty members at Smith College, including myself, hosted an academic session at the college with Martin Niemoeller, the distinguished German Lutheran pastor, who was visiting the campus. We pointed to the failure of the German churches to oppose Adolf Hitler, tracing the roots of this timidity, as we had learned at graduate school, back to Martin Luther's reliance on the German princes in his struggles with the papacy and also forward to the modern church's dependence upon the state for its financial support through taxes.

In response Niemoeller freely admitted that the German churches lacked prophetic courage. However, he then pointed out to his young audience (largely Protestant teachers) that American church leaders do not escape temptation by living in a society that separates church and state. The American churches do not receive tax money, but they instead depend heavily on the donations of their members, particularly their wealthy members, to survive. Their particular moral test is not the dictator's bark of command but the sweet talk of money. At that time Niemoeller saw this problem as being particularly acute for the Protestant churches in the United States as they faced the civil rights struggle and the issue of poverty. The Catholic Church enjoyed substantial discretionary funds available at the diocesan and national levels to respond to the civil rights crisis.[5] However, the major Protestant free churches too often failed to venture beyond the moral predilections of the local congregation.

During the expansion of Protestant churches at the local level in the 1950s, the prophetic task of the ministry tended to give way to the delivery of pastoral services, which ministers owed in any case to their members. Too divisive a response to a particular social or political issue would get in the way of pastoring. Ministers could not afford to offend. Meanwhile, the work of prophecy fell to the national offices of the denominations operating on dwindling budgets, to specialized ministries engaged in social action, or to retired ministers. Such specialized projects targeting social action were important, but they did not usually set the agenda for the local congregation.

Nevertheless, two traditional activities continued (even in a quiescent period) to provide some basis for the church's eventual recovery of its public responsibilities. First, church social services to the sick, the poor, the stranger, and the bereft (following, for example, Hurricane Katrina) can, in addition to their direct benefit, directly remind some Christians that personal works of charity in a market-driven world do not fully suffice to address the basic structural needs of a world the church is called to serve. Second, many congregations, by engaging in the task of self-governance, cultivate some of the habits important to citizenship. They function as deliberative assemblies. In their own internal life as churches, members assume some of the burdens and acquire some of the skills that go with public performance. While the church does not directly aim to cultivate its members as citizens, participation in congregational life pulls parishioners toward the practices of the civic self. They learn something about the art of acting in concert with others for the common good. Churches are among those "intermediate institutions," as the sociologists put it—neither the government nor individual citizens—upon which the health and vigor of a democracy depends.

The African American churches emerged as by far the most historically significant Protestant public force in the twentieth century. When I was a white boy growing up in Houston, Texas, I did not anticipate this development. The black church seemed a pocket of religious life set apart from the larger public reality of the city. Its hymns seemed to celebrate an otherworldly "Beulah Land"; its Sunday sermons offered a religious release from the burdens of the previous week. Its ministers enjoyed a celebrity status but in a strictly confined religious community. Only its women signaled a public life to come for their community that I did not yet understand. Their grand Sunday apparel, especially their hats, crowned a public space that they proudly inhabited, even though they spent their days in their uncrowned labors as servants. At that time in the South black women earned a dollar a day for daylong services. Before World War II their husbands had occasional yard work. As part of the deal, the white employer might make available the room over the family's garage for the servant who was childless or whose children were cared for by a grandparent. More often, workers in Houston, as in other southern cities, boarded buses with clearly marked public space in the front of the bus reserved for whites, whether they occupied that space or not. Blacks, who depended more than whites on public transportation, had to keep behind the color line, sitting or standing, no matter how long their day.

That was the black church then, as seen from outside and at a distance by this white boy—except for the occasion in my mid-teens when I gave a talk at a black church on an unpaved street in a black neighborhood. A black man in the congregation offered a few Amens to help me along. I was startled and caught the Amens awkwardly. They seemed a break in my prepared speech rather than a gift to help me connect with the assembly.

Ten years later, Rosa Parks crossed the racial boundary on a bus and sat down in an unoccupied space, signaling that the bus was a public place and not a priority space for whites. Ten years after that, leaders in the black community, with the help of the courts and television and eventually civil rights legislation, began to enlarge public space to include drinking fountains and parks and bathrooms and schools and higher education and voting booths and restaurants and some jobs and eventually some white neighborhoods and churches—and at length, more than forty years later, the White House.

Having an African American president signaled much more than whites' making room for the excluded in national life. Along with President Obama came a medley of gifts, some of them intermixed with gifts already in the black churches: community organizing; a rhetoric that connects; a refusal to be discouraged; some reading of Martin Luther King Jr. and Reinhold Niebuhr on power politics; some experience in making alliances with urban Catholics on the care of the poor, and therefore some measure of confidence in faith-based initiatives in the unfolding of the country toward a better future; and finally, a temperament disposed toward inclusiveness, with an instinct for reaching out even while moving in—into the White House.

Meanwhile, many Protestant fundamentalists, along with some (by no means all) conservative evangelicals, took up politics, gathering momentum from the mid-1970s forward. They collaborated with leaders of the Republican Party, whose ready-made religion was dualistic. Kevin Phillips, early shaper of the Republican "silent majority" and later rueful critic of the party, warned that the Republican Party became "America's first religious party."[6] The religion in question was not Christian monotheism—but it was certainly religion, and it was anything but marginalized. In collaboration with the

Republican Party, these religionists engaged for forty years in what they defined as a cultural war against evil. They also allied themselves with the devotees of a free market capitalism, tolerating little criticism of the self-correcting and wealth-producing prowess of the marketplace.

In the course of time a second, contrary voice sounded in the conservative evangelical movement. James Wallis founded the Sojourners movement (1971) and eventually the *Sojourners* magazine; then he published half a dozen books, including *God's Politics: Why the Right Gets It Wrong and the Left Doesn't Get It* (2004).[7] With a flair for chapter titles like newspaper headlines, Wallis opposed the Iraq war ("Not a Just War: Mistake of Iraq") and held to a liberal position on economic and welfare issues ("Isaiah's Platform: Budgets Are Moral Documents"). Like the neo-orthodox theologians Paul Tillich and Niebuhr, Wallis mixed theology with a social gospel ethic. But he showed far more interest and confidence than Tillich or Niebuhr in equipping the church itself for a role in public life. Wallis and colleagues provided a minor, but not isolated, voice in the evangelical movement.

In the main body of its teachings the Roman Catholic Church has never deferred as readily as Lutherans to the power of the state to coerce, nor has it enthused as uncritically as Protestant individualists over the prodigality of an unregulated marketplace. The classic Catholic doctrine of a just war carefully limits the conditions under which a government might declare and wage a war justly. The US Catholic bishops' 1983 pastoral letter titled *The Challenge of Peace* perceptively brought this doctrine to bear on military policies of deterrence in a nuclear age. The Church's classical doctrine of a just wage and a just price calls for the protection of workers and their families against the moral indifference of the laws of supply and demand in the marketplace. Carrying forward this tradition in a world suffering today from chronic or severe cycles of unemployment, Pope John Paul II emphasized the importance of human participation in work (*Laborem exercens*, 1981). In response to inequalities of wealth in the latter half of the twentieth century, the US Catholic bishops in 1986 issued another pastoral letter, this time on distributive justice, *Economic Justice for All*, from which individualists still have much to learn. The generally robust Catholic sense of human solidarity does not permit the church to fall into the trap of a bourgeois Protestant individualism that has lost sight of humanity's common condition, plight, and prospect. Catholic Charities has mobilized a commitment far beyond the doctrinal, both lay and clerical, in carrying out corporal works of mercy directed to the common good.[8]

In political debates today, both conservative and progressive Catholics have appealed to the notion of the sacredness of life, but they have drawn different conclusions at the level of political judgment and voting. Conservatives have tended to judge politicians exclusively by their commitment to a pro-life standard and to apply that standard restrictively to the questions of birth control, abortion, stem cell research, homosexual behavior, and same-sex marriage. Progressives have not generally contested the sacredness of life, but they argue that its sacredness also has bearing on the issues of capital punishment, the conduct of war, and economic injustices that tear asunder the human family.

In the 2008 election Catholic progressives argued that a culture of life must reach out to the totality of Catholic teaching: "A culture of life is necessarily connected with a family wage, universal health insurance and, yes, better parenting and education of youth."[9] Politicians fall short of that comprehensive standard if they outdo rivals in backing pro-life Supreme Court appointments while opposing tax policies that might help pregnant women bear and support their children.

Commenting on single-issue debate and politics, M. Cathleen Kaveny of the University of Notre Dame Law School noted that conservative Catholics have dismissed other considerations by singling out such acts as abortion, euthanasia, and homosexual congress as "intrinsic evils"—that is, deliberate actions whose object is objectively evil. While not contesting that definition, Kaveny pointed out that designating an act as intrinsically evil "does not by itself say anything about the comparative gravity of the act. Some acts that are not intrinsically evil (driving while intoxicated) can on occasion be worse both objectively and subjectively than acts that are intrinsically evil (telling a jocose lie). Pronouncing an act or policy an intrinsic evil should not constitute a trump card in forming the political conscience of Catholic citizens."[10] Exit polls after the

2008 election suggested that a majority of Catholics (54 percent) acted on that judgment in casting their votes.[11] In debates over the reform of health care, national organizations of Catholic hospitals, nurses, and others have also backed such reform despite opposition from more restrictive interpreters of the pro-life principle. The debate goes on.

BANKROLLING THE MEDIA

Radio and television have probably formed political culture more directly today than the academy or the churches have. The original expansion of capitalism depended upon a culture of disciplined work, savings, investment, and productivity, but the continuance of capitalism also requires a strong appetite for the products it creates. An economy of supply without demand does not work. At length, however, the indulgence of voracious appetites at the back end seems to sap resources, energy, and requisite discipline at the front end. The margins of resilience for renewal dwindle. "In the world of capitalist enterprise, the nominal ethos in the spheres of production and organization is still of work, delayed gratification, career orientation, devotion to the enterprise. Yet on the marketing side, the sale of goods packaged in the glossy images of glamour and sex, promotes a hedonistic way of life, whose promise is the voluptuous gratification of the lineaments of desire."[12]

The media serve as the primary instrument for whetting the appetites in the consumerist phase of a capitalist society. Until the 1840s, newspapers depended upon the patronage of governments, political parties, and merchant guilds in seaports for their economic base. But technical developments in the mid-nineteenth century led to the penny press and its potential for reaching a mass audience of readers. Advertisers replaced direct patrons such as political parties in the funding of newspapers. The basic purpose of journalism shifted. The Constitution anticipates the reader as citizen; the marketplace pursues the reader as consumer. The First Amendment of the Constitution associates readers with their civil liberties and politics—the difficult art of acting in concert with others for the public good—whereas the marketplace directs the reader or the viewer toward private consumption. The Constitution aims to foster deliberation and the clarification of judgment; the marketplace aims at generating, directing, and gratifying desire. Entertainment (in the sense of finding the story line that will play) replaces information and judgment as the professional ideal. The media have also redefined as somewhat more passive the recipients of news, especially in the arena of politics. They "clue in" their readers to the day's events, treating them as passive spectators and not as active agents. A community composed entirely of onlookers evanesces into what the prophetic Søren Kierkegaard called a "phantom" community. The public is that "abstract whole formed in the most ludicrous way by all participants becoming a third party (an onlooker)." Kierkegaard recognized (more than a century before Neil Postman in *Amusing Ourselves to Death*) that such spectators, who bear no continuing personal responsibility for actions or events, inevitably seek amusement: "This indolent mass which. . . . does nothing itself, this gallery is on the lookout for distraction and soon abandons itself to the very idea that everything that anyone does is done in order to give it (the public) something to gossip about."[13]

Denying responsibility for what they see, spectators look to print and screen voyeuristically. They judge the passing parade of athletes, actors, politicians, and celebrities as performers. All fields slump into entertainment, politics included. By the 2008 election the media were offering round-the-clock reports on who was winning, who was likely to win, and what horse had lost ground since the last report to spectators. The imperial self in question here is not the emperor in the coliseum, the patron of the games, but the spectators in the stands, who have disembodied themselves as citizens.

Deliberation—which takes time—suffers. Politics in a republic traditionally depends upon the capacity of citizens to follow in a newspaper or pamphlet, if only roughly, an extended line of reasoning that consummates in political judgments. But the media encourage impatience with complexity and ambiguity. *USA Today*, following television and preceding the Internet, led the way in the art of abbreviating. Stories have shrunk to a couple of sentences, not much longer than the headlines that draw attention to them. The stories are all head and little body. None of the packaging alarms consumers on the hunt for fast-food stories to go with a fast-food lunch. Such franchised deep-fat tidbits do not provoke reflection to help citizens in a democracy reach complex judgments about issues fateful for the common good.

On the whole, the pressure to simplify ideas has diminished the moderating role of political parties in America and encouraged a single-issue politics. Political parties have traditionally taken some of the hard edge off the combative position of a particular interest group, as parties organized various constituencies into a comprehensive political program. Today, candidates instead desperately need access to expensive media, and they therefore look to well-financed single-issue interest groups to win their party's nomination. Every politician tends to become his or her own political party; fundraisers become deferential to sponsoring lobbyists. Party discipline weakens, with consequences not only for the tenor of political campaigns but for the quality of governance to follow.

That is only part of the story. Quite possibly, the recently developed and much heralded campaign "interactivity" in 2008 may reverse the long decline in the citizen's participation in politics. The Internet, social media, and instant text messaging may help shift the citizen from onlooker to active agent in support of enduring political change. The debate over the relative likelihood of that prospect currently haunts campaign managers and the blogosphere. Clearly, winning an election will not by itself supply an answer. The Internet's interactivity may lead only to short, fevered, reactive spurts rather than to a more sustained engagement in politics. The mechanisms of YouTube and the rest of the Internet may not suffice to convert restless, hungry, occasional players into long-term participants in American politics. Such staying power requires structures in place, not just frenetic activity in cyberspace. Leaders and citizens alike will need the virtues of endurance as well as attack in facing the contrary winds that inevitably will resist efforts to redirect our national appetites.

Meanwhile, managers of the great cable and television networks rely on runaway fear and desire to supply them with the story lines that draw their audiences and keep their patrons paying the bills.

CURBING RUNAWAY APPETITES
IN AMERICAN DOMESTIC POLICY

Oil and Other Carbons

In the course of Rome's decline the wide-eyed Saint Augustine saw Carthage and the imperial city as a "cauldron of illicit loves."[1] In his account of the waning middle ages, the historian Johan Huizinga reported on the carnival appetites that raged in continental Europe.[2] In response to the "snarl of the abyss" beneath the late 1930s, the poet W. H. Auden supplied a somewhat more proper English image for escape: His countrymen enjoyed a "jolly picnic on the heath / Of the agreeable."[3] Following 9/11, Auden's characteristically modest British metaphor yielded to a more colorful fantasy on the American scene. The president of the United States counseled the nation, "Get down to DisneyWorld in Florida. . . . Take your families and enjoy life, the way we want it to be enjoyed."[4]

The president's advice seemed odd if the threat to America was as great as the president painted it, and it seemed unjust because the full burden of defense would fall entirely on volunteer soldiers. However, President George W. Bush appealed to something deep and abiding in his sense of the American character. Get grounded in your basic appetites, he seemed to say: "Enjoy life the way we want it to be enjoyed." What better way to remind people of the world out there to be enjoyed than a pilgrimage to DisneyWorld, a dream world, to be sure, but one not entirely removed from the American dream with which we connect daily by shopping.

On September 18, 2001, the defense secretary at the time, Donald Rumsfeld, spelled out the hard foreign policy implications of this advice for furthering the new order of the ages: "We have two choices. Either we change the way we live or we must change the way they live, and we choose the latter."[5] Changing the way they lived meant war, at first against al-Qaeda and Afghanistan and soon thereafter against Iraq, with the intent of transforming the Middle East and the Islamic world. Meanwhile, however, the American way of life, driven by its appetites, would remain unchanged. Its dreams would suffer no let or limit by taxes, trade deficits, national debt, regulations, mortgages, credit card debt, or national needs for new schools, bridges, light rails, sea walls, or flood controls. Not even the ruination of one of the country's oldest cities by flood in Hurricane Katrina in 2005 halted the picnic on the heath of the agreeable. The sky fell again with the collapse of the financial system in yet another September, in 2008, and oil poisoned the underside of the country in the spring of 2010 with the breaching of the floor of the Gulf of Mexico.

Nothing has more profoundly affected the way we live in the last one hundred years in the United States of America than oil.[6] It has supplied the energy that drives the American way of life from cars to careers to food on the table in a home of one's own. This chapter considers our dependency on oil as it has coursed through our appetites. The focus on oil is not arbitrary or driven by the headlines issuing from the catastrophe in the Gulf. The great empires in the modern world—which have lasted up to 120 or 130 years each—have depended upon a primary supply of energy to power them. They have tended to decline when they have depleted or failed to replace competitively their great energy source. The United States is now ninety to one hundred years into its depletion of oil.

I dedicate this chapter to the owner of the Ford Agency in Cleveland, Ohio, back in the late 1950s. When I expressed worries about the miles per gallon achieved by the eight-cylinder station wagon, which I was circling with the thought of buying, he conceded that the car was a "little thirsty," an admission that subtly challenged whether I was man enough to meet its needs. I bought it.

THE ADDICTION TO OIL

During the Republican Convention of 2008 the chant of "Drill, Baby, Drill" ran through the delegates as a reaction to gasoline prices of four dollars a gallon. Purportedly, drilling for oil both off-shore and on the Alaskan tundra would lower prices at the pump and secure some measure of independence from the troublesome Middle East. Never mind the math in promoting that strategy: A dozen years would pass before this particular yield of oil could possibly influence energy prices at all. The solution would also mindlessly increase our own long-term dependence on foreign oil by drawing down our own scant resources. The United States controls only 3 percent of the world's oil reserves while consuming annually almost 25 percent of the world's yearly energy production. In the absence of changes in American habits and sources of energy, extra drilling would resolutely compound the problem. The tactic resembles the plight of the alcoholic who relies on alcohol to escape his or her problems and then drinks even more to escape the problems created by drinking.

The example of alcholism highlights an important feature of addiction. At first, alcohol enhances pleasures and offers temporary relief from old aggravations and sorrows. However, in the course of time, as the favored and favoring substance becomes the organizing principle around which everything else turns, the addict's world shrinks to pursuing it. Instead of heightening pleasures, alcohol narrows them to its own particular generosity; instead of tamping down pain, it generates its own list of woes; instead of expanding powers, it disables them.

The habit disables the addict directly but also indirectly as it alters the universe that the addict inhabits. The altered world seems to place remedy beyond reach. Jobs are lost or exchanged for loser jobs; marriages break up; and a child's respect dwindles as the child seeks to protect him- or herself against further disappointment at the parent's stumbling. Addicts find it difficult to make sober assessments of both their objective plight and their complicity in it. Addicts obscure for themselves the price they have paid for a world that increasingly narrows to their habit.

The US addiction to oil has become a diagnostic cliché. In his 2006 State of the Union address, President Bush reported to the nation, "Here we have a serious problem; America is addicted to oil, which is often imported from unstable parts of the world."[7] The last half of the president's sentence exposes a deep fault in part of his remedy—a bold plan to straighten things out with a war in the Middle East. It is as if a doctor warned an alcoholic patient that the liquor came from a dangerous neighborhood and advised the patient to drink up what was left in the house while the doctor cleaned up the neighborhood to secure again the supply. Since cleaning up the Middle East was not working out well, the president briefly looked to the long-range future and prophesied the eventual development of nuclear and hydrogen energy. However, Bush made no serious commitment of federal funds to these (or other) long-term projects. In effect, he let the nation settle back into its routines, its habits of consumption unaltered. That is the moment in a decision when the devil lights up a victory cigar. He knows he has won. As Søren Kierkegaard observed, the devil does not care how much you talk about changing tomorrow or twenty years from now, as long as you give him today.

THE PRICE OF ADDICTION

Experts in foreign policy have long warned of the price America pays for its addiction to oil. To slake our thirst we transfer billions of petrodollars a year to the dictators of oil-producing nations, and we have indebted ourselves to China and other nations to bankroll our very expensive habit. The price will only go higher for a nation so massively dependent on oil. We are rapidly depleting our domestic source. The world's supply will peter out in thirty or forty years. As Karl Menninger wrote in *Man against Himself*, alcoholism is a kind of suicide by inches. A superpower so fixedly dependent upon oil will more likely die by guzzling down the oil barrel than by looking down the gun barrel.

Environmentalists have measured the further costs of our (and the world's) addiction to oil: the dangerous pollutants that we pump into the air; the physical assaults of spills, leaks, and blowouts; and the debilitating impacts of the automobile on the underexercised human body. In 2006 Terry Tamminen toted up the various costs in reduced crop yields, increased health care costs, and damages to buildings, forests, and water. To these costs he added the annual tax breaks and subsidies enjoyed by the oil and gas industries (at a time when six oil companies ranked among the fifteen top companies on the Fortune Global 500) and arrived at an estimated cost ranging up to $806 billion a year.[8] The tax breaks enjoyed by the oil and gas industries, including most obviously the "depletion allowance," hugely favor this extractive industry over other kinds of manufacturing that receive no tax breaks in anticipation of a diminishing supply of materials. Tamminen's figure also did not include the additional impacts on global warming that Americans and all the world's inhabitants will face if the West and the emergent powers of India and China do not find some way of sobering up in the face of runaway habits.

Attention to the issue of energy has waxed and waned with the rise and fall in the cost of gasoline since the 1970s, but the catastrophic event on April 20, 2010, put the issue back on the front page. Oil gushed from the blowout of a new well drilled by British Petroleum (BP) in the Gulf of Mexico a mile under water and fifty miles off the shore of Louisiana. (The state has already lost surface area the size of the state of Delaware through various environmental impacts since 1932.) The BP disaster killed eleven people. Three weeks later, it was continuing to contaminate the Gulf at varying estimates of twenty to thirty thousand (and eventually many more) barrels of oil a day. The event threatened to demolish the fishing, shrimp, and tourist industries. In congressional hearings on May 12, 2010, the relevant companies—British Petroleum; Transocean, owner and operator of the rig; and Halliburton, responsible for cementing the hole—warily attempted to blame one another or downplay the disaster. Government agencies for once were blamed for regulating too little, not too much.

In the setting of the emergency Senators John Kerry (D-MA) and Joe Lieberman (I-CT) unveiled a compromise energy and climate bill known as the American Power Act. In addition to provisions for carbon reduction and the development of renewable energy sources, the proposal would permit some (highly regulated) initiatives in nuclear power and offshore drilling. The bundle of centrist proposals differs from Bush's in that the government would put serious money into renewable energy programs and thus would recognize the provisional status of drilling for oil as the country turns itself around. Little progress is likely to be made on such legislation following the congressional elections of November 2010.

DEALING WITH ADDICTION

Some critics have dealt with the oil addiction by delivering jeremiads against the oil and gas industries and related allies, such as the tire and highway construction industries, that profit from a bad habit. The record certainly justifies such attacks. The American Automobile Manufacturers Association did all that it could to "delay research, development, manufacturing and installation" of devices to control toxic exhaust and lung damage.[9] It stalled on installing catalytic converters on cars and trucks, and it fought to kill the development of zero emission vehicles. It resisted state and national gas mileage standards. The American Petroleum Institute opposed cleaner standards for diesel-powered buses and better regulations on the emission of ozone in the air (partly on the grounds that people get used to it).[10] Further, these industries opposed mass transportation so as to deprive the public of another option in travel. (Notoriously, in 1922 Alfred Sloan Jr., leading General Motors, bought up companies and removed streetcars from the city of Los Angeles, a strategy eventually repeated in forty-five cities with the enthusiastic cooperation of the oil, truck, and highway industries, thus making way for the clogged highways and smogged skies of the future.)[11] The record justifies a serious attack on the policies promulgated by these industries and the development of remedies directed to the common good.

However, an attack that focuses entirely on a set of enablers or exploiters misses the depth of the problem and postpones remedy. It leaves the addiction firmly in place. Blame the exploiters. Treat the addict as innocent victim. Addicts thrive on the passive voice. The fault lies elsewhere, not with me or with us. Determined exploiters, of course, indulge in a different kind of moral passivity. They testify before Congress that the market obliges them to give the public what it wants, while they ignore the billions of dollars they have zealously spent over the years in generating and manipulating those wants.

While exploiters surely bear substantial responsibility, the addict's recovery also requires an act of self-recognition. It requires owning up to an appetite deep within the psyche, a kind of imperial thirst for a life without limits in which the self is deeply complicit. Recovery also requires recognizing the degree to which the long-term addiction has massively reconfigured the outer world in which the addict finds himself. The future does not offer people effortless access to a delete key or a reset button.

The internal combustion machine remade the world. The advent of the car offered a draft of liberty, the gift of power and speed behind the wheel. Young men exulted in it instantly—the automobile, a self-driven vehicle that rescues the driver from fellow passengers on a streetcar or train and from train schedules, a power so wondrous as to be measured in huge multiples of horsepower and so beneficent as to leave no trace of waste in the streets. The car also let young couples escape congested apartment living in the cities and fulfill the dream of a home of their own in the suburbs, distant from the soot and grime of the industrial cities in which their immigrant parents had worked. It signaled a fresh start for their children and themselves, unencumbered by the past.

In the course of time the dream has produced a carbon waste that wreaks its havoc on the planet, and it causes suburbanites to waste time in daily commuting that weakens and strains the nuclear family. The dream has also objectively reconfigured the landscape in ways difficult to reverse. We say that we should invest more money in mass transportation—undeniably so, but mass transportation works if commuters live within walking or cycling distance of the bus, trolley, or subway stop. Unfortunately, most cities and suburbs expanded with cars, not sidewalks or bike lanes, in mind. Homes and yards sprawled out in every direction. Only the car, or several of them, in the garage-attached house could deliver people to work or school or mall—or to the fitness center, where bipeds might recover some of their aboriginal skills as walkers.

THE FURTHER REACH OF OIL

Oil and petrochemicals have reconfigured the landscape in other ways even more dramatic than urban sprawl. Petrochemicals have spectacularly increased the world's food supply. In the mid-1940s Norman Borlaug, the eventual Nobel Prize winner known as the father of the "green revolution," went to Mexico and developed, with the help of pesticides and fertilizers, disease-resistant varieties of wheat with spectacularly increased yields. He and others improved strains of rice and corn in other famished parts of the world. At his death on September 12, 2009, Borlaug was credited with having saved one billion people from starvation.

At nearly the same time, however, a countercultural "green movement" began as a protest against the green revolution. Michael Pollan notes that, in the same decade in which Borlaug initiated his work, Sir Albert Howard published *An Agricultural Testament* (1943), which eventually served as the bible for the reaction to the industrialization of agriculture. Without contesting that petrochemicals have spectacularly increased the world's food supply, the protest movement has warned that synthetic fertilizer would destroy diversity and open the way to all the vulnerabilities of a monoculture. "Instead of eating exclusively from the sun, humanity now began to sip petroleum."[12] And sip it fast.

The phrase "fast food" today describes not simply the speed with which a restaurant serves it up or we gulp it down but also the hurried growth of food from egg to chicken to pot. "In the nineteen-seventies, it took ten weeks to raise a broiler, now it takes forty days in a dark and crowded shed."[13] Pig factories, animal feed lots, and single-crop landscapes of soy and corn have replaced the diversified farms of a half century ago. As agriculture has industrialized, farm workers have dropped from 40 percent to 2 percent of the US population. Supermarkets and box stores bulge with staples shipped in from elsewhere and are sold at prices that have driven out of business the ma-and-pa stores that once gave coherence and texture to town squares.

Meanwhile, America itself has become a huge box store that imports staples and generic manufactured goods from all over the world. Poor countries depend upon a single crop or an extractive industry that pulls their populations from subsistence farming into the cities. The survival of countries dangles from decisions made elsewhere in the United States or northern Europe, and the altered local economy forfeits the food safety net that diversity helped keep in place. A single crop or market failure can expose a region or nation to instant disaster.

Thus, despite the spectacular increases in agricultural productivity that insecticides, fertilizers, and oil and diesel fuels have brought about (achievements that would astonish Thomas Robert Malthus), some 800 million people on the planet went to bed hungry in 2006. A final irony accompanies that figure. While 800 million people were hungry, another billion were overweight. The hungry are the poor, but the poor are also among the larger population of the overweight who cannot afford or do not choose to eat fresh produce. The coexistence of obesity and hunger warn that relying solely on a market-driven system for ordering the human appetites can leave much else awry.

The moral of the story hardly concludes in a plea for blanket federal interventions from the top down. Government research, after all, contributed mightily to the welcome huge increases in productivity in the twentieth century. However, the United States Department of Agriculture (USDA) also encouraged small-scale experiments in better farming that caught on, largely through research at agricultural and mechanical (A&M) universities and through its network of county extension agents. Those interventions differed markedly from the later huge price supports for agribusinesses that completed the industrialization of agriculture. Continuing aid for research and field experiments will be needed to realize fully the benefits of such ventures as organic farming and to guide the processing of food in such a way as to not addict children to sugar at the breakfast table.

Meanwhile, the urbane Mayor Michael Bloomberg of New York has campaigned against trans-fatty acids and showed the way toward more public discipline in our appetites. More generally, the surgeon Atul Gawande outlined a lesson for health care in what has transpired in agriculture: the need for government support for experimental field projects in better health care, and the dissemination of such knowledge in such a way as to help counter current runaway practice. These are relatively unnoticed features of the proposals incorporated into health care reform in 2010.[14]

AUGUSTINE CONSIDERS THE APPETITES

Were we to view the cities of New York and Washington today with the eyes of the young, ambitious Augustine making his way in Milan or in the imperial city of Rome, we would sound at first like a modern preacher, inveighing against the gross materialism of our appetites. Augustine's phrase "lust of the flesh" covers all those goods of touch, taste, and smell on which the heart feasts in gratifying its own immediate wants. However, Augustine resorted to a second phrase, the "spectacle of the eyes," to capture the aesthetic dazzle and allure of a great city: the shine of its arts, the beauty and proportion of its buildings, the luxurious color of its clothing and language. Still further, Augustine recognized that a city holds out a prospect, yet more spacious and grand than either the lust of the flesh or a spectacle for the eyes. It offers a possible glory in performance and accomplishment that rewards those who master it with goods not available in the provinces—a level of command and control, honor and acclaim, a way of life in the imperial city that Augustine summarized with the phrase the "pride of life" (book 10, nos. 30–43).

From Saint Augustine forward, the Catholic Christian tradition has located and celebrated the *humanum* in the power of desire, but the tradition has not defined appetite itself as evil. Augustine, for example, distinguished humans from all other creatures by virtue of their experience at the very core of their being of an infinite and boundless thirst. The needs of the beast are limited. The animal wants food, sleep, and the satisfaction of its flesh; and it sets out to meet those needs without embarrassment or complication. But humans know a surplus of desire above and beyond all these satisfactions. They do not live contentedly within limits. At the very height of their pleasures humans are thrown beyond them, whether by boredom, satiety, or an uneasy awareness of their brevity.

For Augustine this surplus of desire signals both the grandeur and the misery of humankind. In grandeur of origin and destiny God intended humans for the satisfaction of their boundless desire.

God did not sadistically burden humans with an infinite passion in order to thwart it. God created humans for happiness rather than unhappiness, satisfaction rather than torture. Since an infinite passion can be satisfied only by an infinite object, humans must have been created for the purpose of satisfaction in the infinite God, whose unbounded goodness, life, and power alone can provide them with perfect nourishment and rest.

This very desire, however, roils the waters when humans attempt to satisfy it with finite goods. They turn to the limited, transient, and mortal, trying to slake a thirst for the eternal. Looking back over his own past, Augustine recorded in the *Confessions* how he had pursued one good after another, wild with desire, seeking God, painfully and mistakenly, in everything he touched. Despite his high ambition and achievements he was no better off than a drunken beggar whom he saw passing along a street in Milan: "For here was I striving away, dragging the load of unhappiness under the spurring of my desires, and making it worse by dragging it: and with all our striving, our one aim was to arrive at some sort of happiness without care: the beggar had reached the same goal before us, and we might never reach it at all . . .—namely the pleasure of a temporary happiness—I was plotting for with many a weary twist and turn. Certainly the beggar's joy was no true joy, but the joy I sought in my ambition was emptier still" (book 6, no. 6).

Augustine's epiphanic moment illumined the addictions of his own civilization in the course of its waning, and yet another civilization still in the making. His insight differed from rival accounts of the human plight. Humans need not extinguish desire as such. The finite goods of food, clothing, shelter, drink, friendship, love, work, and the arts derive from God; they should be savored and honored as gifts from God. However, when humans pursue such goods ravenously in place of God, they subject both the goods to which they turn and themselves to a double torture. They badger and exhaust the goods by loading them with a burden they cannot bear. They act like the parent who lays on a child the demand for an extravagant accomplishment to atone for the parent's own mediocre achievements. By the same token humans torture themselves; they let themselves in for a letdown. The goods to which they turn cannot abate the craving, no more than the child to whom the parent turns for meaning can possibly quench the parent's extravagant thirst.

Augustine's beggar (and Augustine, who recognized himself in the derelict's plight) illumined his own civilization and perhaps our own in the course of its waning. He gave us a memorable phrase, "a licking after shadows." An addicted nation drains its dwindling supply of oil like a child sucking up more air than soda from the bottom of a straw. In its dereliction the addicted nation flogs its hillsides for coal; beribbons its valleys with asphalt highways; pollutes its common supply of air, water, and earth; deregulates its markets; rewards 5 percent of its population with control over much of its wealth; defers the repair of its frayed infrastructure; starves and neglects its schools; and runs its economic system into the ground.

THE APPETITES IN THE SETTING OF ANXIETY

The Augustinian account of the appetites does not complete the story in the West. Auden called our era the "age of anxiety." When asked at a public meeting that I attended what date he would mark as the beginning of the age of anxiety, Auden replied, "Shakespeare's *Hamlet*." The play dramatizes the human soul befogged with anxiety, disconnected from its bearings, inwardly divided. *Hamlet* describes the adolescent perplexed, his desires awry, his will adrift: "the native hue of resolution / is sicklied o'er with the pale cast of thought" (3:1). The play also catches the anxious, guilty king at prayer: "My words fly up, my thought remain below: / Words without thoughts never to heaven go" (3:3).

It can be also be argued that the classical Protestants around the time of William Shakespeare helped shift examination of the religious plight from desire to anxiety. Whereas the Catholic tradition from Augustine forward interpreted human life under the aspect of desire and its satisfaction, the classical Protestants sited humans in the setting of anxiety and the quest for assurance. Martin Luther recognized that anxiety shows up in a ceaseless effort to justify oneself by one's good works to secure communion with God.

Luther tried every means available to him as a priest to assure himself of God's favor—through the sacraments and sacramentals and through scrupulous efforts to obey the Ten Commandments and the Sermon on the Mount. However, his efforts only served to multiply his doubts. Jesus said, "Do not be anxious about your life" (Mt 6:25). But measured against this standard and many other commandments, who could escape condemnation? Luther was among the unrighteous. And even when he succeeded in obeying the law, he found himself once again falling, this time into the sins not of the unrighteous but of the self-righteous. His good works availed no more than his evil works in securing the presence of God.

All his efforts at salvation through his own works actually removed him further from the presence of God. They were all headed in the wrong direction. They were efforts at self-justification. They only served to drive him deeper into himself, away from God and his neighbor, as he feverishly tried through his good works to secure some sort of divine favor. Meanwhile, God himself became more and more the hidden enemy, the inscrutable X, whom he anxiously tried to appease.

Turning to scripture, Luther discovered that God, as he has actually made himself known in his promises, does not lurk in the future as an X upon whom creatures wait uneasily. Rather, God has already spoken an unmovable word of assurance to sinners that their sins are forgiven and that all grounds for their anxiety before God have been set aside.

Because this is the case, humans can set aside all the little stratagems of anxiety. In Luther's time this meant that humans could put aside all those actions they previously performed so feverishly or indolently to win God's favor. In modern times it means that humans can afford to set aside their own preferred means of self-justification: the piling up of money, the triumph of a career, the moisture in their passions, and the subtlety of their opinions. Having put aside all these works, stripped clean of everything except the assurance of God's grace, humans can begin to live freely and lightheartedly, obedient to God and servant to the neighbor. In brief, assurance is not an uncertain destination but the indispensable, wholly surprising, and merciful point of departure in the Christian life.

Neither Luther nor other reformers explicitly reinterpreted the common human plight in the context of anxiety alone. It remained for theologians of the nineteenth and twentieth centuries to do this.

Humans turn to goods other than God not so much because they are desirable but because they offer some relief from insecurity. The proud inflate their intellectual, moral, and spiritual attainments; they puff up their résumés, not for the satisfaction they offer as attractive achievements in the foreground but rather for the securities they provide against uncertainties menacing in the background.[15] Consumers stretch to buy the larger house, the prized automobile, or a degree from a more highly rated school less for the intrinsic worth of the good than for the reassurance these acquisitions offer that their possessors belong to a higher social class. According to the economist Robert H. Frank, such "positional" or status goods tend to create a "financial arms race" from the top down.[16] Within this dynamic, the lovelessness of the motive is striking. The gluttonous turn to food; the lustful to sex; the wrathful and the envious to their obsessions with loveless fervor, in order to secure themselves against the impalpable. The diverse faulted human activities are defensive reactions against insecurity more than positive drives toward pleasure.

This book makes no attempt to rank either craving or anxiety above the other as the spring of action in the shaping of American policies. I rely more on the category of fear and anxiety in interpreting issues in foreign affairs from the Cold War through the threat of terrorism. That interpretation carried through in the second chapter's discussion of domestic policy. Free market ideologues have aggressively defended the free market against menacing intrusions by the government and against even the mildest displays of independence from other centers of power. However, ravenous appetite has also played its role in a foreign policy often justified by an ideology that brooks no limits in the acquisition of money, power, and goods in order to defend the American way of life. Fear and craving have also intermixed in domestic policy. In good times the appetites drive the American way of life in decisions about cars, housing, food, debts, and investments, until at length the market's wild ride leads to a crash. The most recent crisis, from September 2008 forward, produced a dramatic shift from heedless prodigality to anxious frugality, from a paroxysm of appetite to the paralysis of fear.

As suggested earlier in the book, John Maynard Keynes interpreted wild swings in the market as following from two species of the love of money. In its irrational exuberance a bull market recklessly pursues the goal of making ever more money. This pursuit is objectless in the sense that it is abstracted from any particular goods that the money might buy. The downward swing of the market shifts into the miser's love of money by guarding against any and all forms of its loss. The miser becomes loathe to spend or lend. A wise government, Keynesians have argued, needs to develop countercyclical fiscal policies: first, to tax and regulate in good times in order to curb the boundless appetite for money that leads to huge inequalities of wealth and ultimately unemployment; and second, to spend in bad times in order to rescue the society from the immobilities of hoarding and distrust.[17] Keynes interpreted both forms of the excessive love of money as objectless and abstract because moneymaking and money hoarding abstracts money from the range of human goods it ought to serve.

The perspective offered by Augustine and the Protestant reformers offers a different take on the last point. Augustine believed that the love of money is abstract and spectral in that it seeks to satisfy an infinite thirst with a finite sop. The pursuit of the "ever more" of money perversely reflects a haunted pursuit of the Infinite beyond all finite objects and thus disorders the proper appreciation and use of finite goods. Alternatively, Protestant theologians like Reinhold Niebuhr and Paul Tillich might recognize the power of anxiety at work in Keynes's distinction between uncertainty and risk. Both Niebuhr and Tillich recognized the way in which humans cover over their deeper existential anxieties by focusing on more controllable fears.[18] The market tends to be driven by a deep uncertainty that presses players to cross borders toward the limitless acquisition of money and power. By devising short-term techniques to manage petty risks, these players obscure for themselves the deeper uncertainties that lie beyond their control.

Long before the intricacies of modern finance, the biblical tradition warned that riches and worries grow together. The Gospel of Luke recounts the story of the rich man whose land brings forth plentifully, and immediately he starts to worry: "What shall I do, for I have nowhere to store my crops?" So he tries to tamp down his worries with a plan. He will tear down his barns and build larger ones to store his grain and goods. And then he fantasizes about the ease that will follow. But of course it never comes, for that night he dies; as for the things he has prepared, "whose will they be?" (Lk 12:20). Who can build silos tall enough to secure heart's ease?

Luke precedes and follows this parable on avarice with an admonition on anxiety: "I tell you, do not worry about your life" (Lk 12:22–34). Scholars have suggested that these two blocks of material, the parable and the admonition, were probably derived from two separate oral traditions about Jesus. (In chapter 6 of his gospel Matthew records the admonition about anxiety but not the parable. The Gospel of Mark reports neither.) Luke puts together these two blocks of teachings together. He sees the relation between greed and worry. Possessions trigger worries about securing one's possessions; and worry organizes the hunt for whatever possessions, in whatever quantity, will tamp down one's worries. Acquisitiveness and anxiety feed one another.

Acquisitiveness and anxiety test America's core identity and fiber as a nation. Two competing story lines are at play in American politics—contractual and covenantal. They partly resemble one another, but they also offer differing accounts of the nation's identity and its ways of accommodating or containing its appetites and fears. The closing three chapters of this book more explicitly explore these shaping narratives.

5

WE THE PEOPLE

A Contract or a Covenant?

There are at least four ways to understand the question of the identity of a people that bear on the American scene: unnatural, natural, contractual, and covenantal. Only the last two figure centrally in this chapter.

By *unnatural* I have in mind an identity imposed upon a people chiefly through violence. The dominating power governs unnaturally in the sense that it rules without the consent of the people and with little attention either to their prior identity or to their current well-being. One thinks inevitably of some myth like the rape of Europa or similar stories of conquest the world over. Such a disaster befell not the settlers in America but rather the Native Americans, whom the settlers and their government humiliated, drove from their natural habitats, and violated with broken treaties and promises.

Traditionally in Western history the concept of a *natural* identity highlights those natural structures that humans seem to share with other creatures—organic, hierarchical, and perhaps patriarchical—which justify aristocratic and/or monarchical orderings of political society. Secular critics argue that this derivation of identity reflected a conservative Catholic and European politics that Americans were eager to shed. However, Catholic theorists have also drawn on the tradition of natural law to highlight those properties and goals humans share by nature that distinguish them from other species. This particular emphasis on natural law leads to an understanding of human nature that transcends any particular identities based on nation, race, gender, class, culture, or custom. It also provides a possible basis for establishing, repairing, moderating, and improving relations between various peoples and national groups.

Whatever the potential benefits of this universalism on the American scene, Roman Catholics, its eventual and chief religious bearers, were not sufficiently numerous or influential at the time of the nation's founding to shape the country's sense of itself. Further, the actual circumstances at the time of the founding made it difficult to identify a common nature that underlies and overpowers particular, discrete ethnic identities. The first motto impressed on the great seal of the United States—*e pluribus unum*—bluntly affirms America to be an *original* plurality. Out of that plurality a unity came into being through some kind of agreement between parties—"from the many, one."

In this respect the eventual United States of America differs from its British and European counterparts. Long before Germany, France, and Great Britain were nations, they were roughly identifiable peoples. Governments grew more or less organically out of what each already was. Identity was natural, not something conceived or fabricated out of natures antecedently multiple. However, immigrants landing in the New World carried with them differing ethnic, cultural, and linguistic identities. They could not draw on an antecedent identity for being an American. Except by conquest, that identity could emerge only through some kind of choice or promissory event.

Two alternatives therefore lay open for interpreting the promissory event in and through which the nation came into being: contractual or covenantal.

A *contractualist* account of American identity emphasizes the importance of choice, pure and simple, in creating a unity that was not there before. Consider again the motto *e pluribus unum*, a phrase that posits an original plurality. In the midst of that plurality a gathering of men in constitutional convention drew up a contract that they felt might satisfy the multiple but perhaps overlapping interests of each. Such an agreement would project the country toward a unity—*e pluribus unum*. So conceived, in the words of the social ethicist Charles Matthewes, "the United States is not a fact, a given reality; it is a destiny, an ideal, a dare, a mission, a matter of goals and ideals."[1] The phrase *e pluribus unum* emphasizes America as a project, a construction out of materials hitherto and perhaps continuingly multiple. Unity (the indispensable condition of identity) results from that construction. National unity issues from a choice. (In a sense the "many," the diverse groups of which Americans were composed, underwent and endured a kind of preparation for this choice. In coming here each group separated itself [or was forcibly separated] from a particular past, often called the "old country," which might be remembered fondly but could not, by itself, constitute the new world into which they entered.) The new world was a construction still under construction.

On the surface a sunny secular optimism seems to accompany this notion of a nation founded on a contract. Immigrants had escaped the burdens and intransigencies of Europe and faced forward into a future guided by that contract. At the same time, however, a built-in pathology lurks in an identity so founded. A nation that comes into being solely through the device of a contract blurts out its own contingency. Its identity is not antecedently grounded. It does not result even in part from the discovery of a reality in which choosers already participate. It comes into being through invention. And choice is rickety! This unease about choice leads to a peculiar preoccupation in American politics with demonstrating the absoluteness of the choice so as to shore up national identity. Otherwise the nation would founder. Nothing less than being 100 percent American will do, and nothing is more lethal than the charge of being un-American. Anxiety throws a long shadow over the identity of the nation and its citizens. Eager to prove their own earnest buy-in, citizens may be particularly tempted to point an accusatory finger toward immigrants, liberals, and other assorted outliers whose customs and choices may seem less than 100 percent pure.

Some have discerned a still darker religious apprehension and pathology underlying a contractualist account of national identity. Anxiety haunts the nation's origins, but not because its identity dangles from wobbly choices. Quite the contrary, a harsh necessity drove the original choice: the utter futility of trying to fend off evils that would afflict individuals in a state of nature without the protection of government.

Historians have recognized this dark background in the thought of Thomas Hobbes, the author of *Leviathan* (1651).[2] The fear of theft, fraud, murder, and conquest drives people together into a compact accepting protection from the state. This menacing account of origins persisted in the narrative account of the social contract offered by the theorist John Locke, whose views carried forward through the eighteenth century. Locke hardly described the state of nature antecedent to government in pastel colors. He recognized the power of the negative that propels the entry into the social contract. Why would a rational, self-interested individual, "absolute lord of his own person and possessions," enter into a contract that requires surrendering some measure of liberty, property, and power to the state? Such individuals would cut the deal because they need the state to protect them from the evils that would beset them apart from the contract. Absent protection, Locke argued, man's life would be "full of fears and continual dangers."[3] Thus humans, "notwithstanding all the privileges of the state of nature, being but in an ill condition while they remain in it, are quickly driven into society."[4] In this sense, government is not simply an unprompted but a *driven* choice. Individuals must forfeit a portion of their life, liberty, and estate and submit to the impositions of government to secure themselves against still greater impositions and evils.

This account of the origins of the state appears to be wholly secular in that it looks to a rational human construct to justify political authority, not to a Supreme Good, such as the divine appointment of kings or to the hierarchical ordering of nature. Nevertheless such a state is religiously driven, in that it derives reflexively from a Supreme Evil: the towering dangers that would beset the self's own interests apart from the protection of government. The self enters into the bargain of creating a government to keep itself intact as a self-interested creature following along the track of its interests and appetites in the midst of otherwise unstoppable peril.

This contractualist account of American identity faces a deep inner flaw. It does not offer a narrative to counter adequately the problems of either runaway fear or appetites. It begins in Locke as a defense of limited government, solely legitimated by its delegated authority to protect against negative threats; but unsteadied and unrestrained by any other source of authority, the government focuses eventually on imminent dangers to justify and expand its powers. At length a fear of the negative can dominate, as the nation preoccupies itself with the fight against the evil du jour—foreign powers, domestic enemies, strangers in the neighborhood, the disease of the month, whatever. A government founded in fear is easy prey to runaway fear.

At the same time, a contractualist account of the nation's origins leaves little resource for curbing runaway appetites. The government comes into being solely through the self's interest in resisting impositions upon itself. Imposing is the supreme evil. The government engages in legitimate imposing, through taxes, to protect against the larger imposings suffered under the conditions of either anarchy or tyranny. Government in this sense is a necessary evil. So justified, however, the government cannot impose taxes and regulations upon its citizens for other purposes. Such mission creep would divert and exhaust resources needed elsewhere. Worse yet, to tax and regulate for other purposes would be perverse. The government would begin to resemble the original evil, which by contract it is obliged to resist.

This contractualist theory postulates the major player in the contract as the ownership self. The government cannot intrude upon the self except for its protection. Locke prepared the way for this understanding of the deep self as owner. He used the word "property" to cover comprehensively all that is one's self, one's *propre*, including one's life, one's liberty, and one's estate (that is, property in the narrower sense). C. B. Macpherson dubbed this political theory "possessive individualism." It rests on the proposition that "the individual is essentially the proprietor of his own person and capacities, for which he owes nothing to society."[5] Later libertarianism would harbor a deep suspicion of any intrusions by regulations and taxes on the ownership self, since the deep self, other than what it has purchased to protect itself, owns itself, lock, stock, and barrel.

It is hardly an accident, three centuries after Locke, that free marketeers, achieving majority control of the US House of Representatives in 1994, would ceremonially promote a Contract with America and hammer incessantly against taxes and regulations. When moreover the Republican party captured the presidency in 2000, it would celebrate the nation as the "ownership society." The slogan of ownership drove its efforts on several fronts: to privatize the social security system; to run student loans through the commercial banking system; to keep health care largely in the hands of for-profit payers and providers; and (along with their Democratic predecessors) to put Americans into homes of their own, whether they could afford them or not. Eventually the collapse of the stock market, the destruction of private retirement accounts, the undermining of a job-based health care system, the deluge of bankruptcy proceedings against both ordinary homeowners and the great corporations, and the huge rise in the numbers of the unemployed tarnished the dream of the ownership society. Overheated appetites yielded to icy fear and panic. A contractualist account of American identity does not fare well in dealing with runaway appetites and fear.

The fourth way of understanding American identity defines it as neither natural/unnatural nor contractual but *covenantal*. "Covenant" is not a term to which the founders appealed. The word crossed the Atlantic much earlier with the Protestant Puritans, some of whom famously entered into a shipboard covenant before landing in Massachusetts. In that setting the word "covenant" describes the self-understanding of a people defined by a promissory event that cuts more deeply into the self and reaches farther into the future than a contract. The origin and well-being of each cannot fully be read apart from the well-being and destiny of all members. Instead of establishing a government reluctantly by forfeit, a covenanted people recognize an element of mutual self-expenditure in their origin.

The original language was explicitly religious. Bound together in the "ligaments of love" is the way John Winthrop expressed the power of the covenantal tie in his shipboard sermon on the *Arbella*.[6] Although Protestants eventually succumbed to the rhetoric of individualism, the early Puritans did not embrace that creed. They were not religious solitaries or political individualists. They recognized themselves as a people covenanted together. They were also not theocrats. They distinguished the religious from the political covenant. The pastor of the church did not serve as the town's magistrate. Both covenants resembled one another in that they saw civil government not as a necessary evil reluctantly established by contract, but rather as the emboldening impetus of their life together as a people, which their covenants affirmed and their enduring purposes projected.

The religious background for the term "covenant" needs to be explored in due course. For the moment, let the word simply stand for a relation that is neither natural/umbilical nor contractual/commercial. A covenantal identity resembles a contract in that it issues from a promissory event. But it differs in that it recognizes a doubleness in that event. The United States is a project, as the motto "out of many, one" emphasizes. However, it announces itself at its very birth as both a reality and a project.

Consider the first words we uttered as a nation: "We the People." The preamble to the Constitution does not begin with a "many" from which a unity is concocted. It does not proclaim, "We, the factions of the United States" or "We, the interest groups of the United States" or "We, the states of the United States" or "We the individuals of the United States"—it proclaims, "We the People." On the face of it, the "We" seems to be not a construct but a reality, acting as the communal agent of a construct that moves beyond its original imperfection toward a more perfect union.

This first phrase recognizes the original gift of life together, "We the People," but a gift swiftly charged with a covenantal task: "in order to form a more perfect Union." We are at once a community but also a community in the making. We are a reality, but also a project.

THE PREAMBLE TO THE CONSTITUTION

Some have argued that the declaration "We the People" is a fiction. According to the economic interpretation of national origins, the propertied classes mounted a revolution to reject the tyranny of taxes imposed from abroad. A decade later they constructed the Constitution with sufficient executive and legislative authority vested in the federal government to protect the country against foreign threats and destructive waves of populism within the country and to provide a reliable framework for commerce between the states. To these ends, fifty-five men of property created a fiction. The "people" purportedly functioned as the agent and protagonist in their playbook—the bible for the nation—that would protect their interests and those of their progeny. These men of property, protecting themselves, simply spoke with a louder voice by saying, "We the People."

Some historians eventually rejected the cruder aspects of Charles A. Beard's economic interpretation of the Constitution.[7] They argued that public-spiritedness, not simply economic self-interest, figured in the decisions of the founders. However, this rebuttal did not retire the scholarly judgment that the preamble to the Constitution begins with a fiction. "It was not 'the people' who clamored for the Constitution, but rather a small elite group of men," asserted the historian Edward Countryman at the end of the twentieth century.[8]

Expanding on this theme the dean of American historians, Edmund S. Morgan, argued that fictions figure across the board in politics: "The success of government . . . requires the acceptance of fictions, requires the willing suspension of disbelief, requires to believe that the emperor is clothed even though he is not." The government of the United States, like other governments, began with make-believe: "Make believe that the king is divine or that he can do no wrong, make believe that the voice of the people is the voice of God. Make believe that the people *have* or that the representatives of the people *are* the people."[9] James Madison, the primary drafter of the American Constitution, seemed to recognize this fabulous element as well. In July 1819 he observed, "The infant periods of most nations are buried in silence, or veiled in fable, and perhaps the world may have lost but little which it need not regret."[10]

An opportunistic account of origins suffers from a difficulty that goes deeper than the historical question as to whether men of property veiled their impure motives in a fiction. (In fact, some of them had exposed themselves to considerable risk by signing the Declaration of Independence. Their signatures on the document amounted to a death warrant should the undertaking fail.) The novelist Flannery O'Connor exposed the deeper difficulty in her account of the role of myths in human affairs. She said, in effect, "You know a people by the stories they tell."[11] O'Connor had in mind, of course, myths, by which she meant stories that coincide with and reinforce human experience. Myths are narratives so deeply true that people repeat them, appeal to them, and act them out. Myths order their expectations and mold sensibilities. They shape people cognitively and morally. Cognitively they give people a vision of their world and themselves. Morally they cue people in, telling them how to behave in the light of these perceptions: They assign them their duties toward themselves and others.

Its mythic power helps explain why the story line of "We the People" in the preamble to the Constitution took hold with Americans—why Americans did not dismiss the story line as a mere fiction, why the preamble supplied them with a preliminary and compressed narrative for which the body of the Constitution furnished the law. The writers themselves were not engaging in pure invention. Some of the founders, including Madison, were well acquainted with the ancients on the subject of the various types of government: monarchical, aristocratic, and republican—government by one, the few, and the many. All could draw on 150 years of experience with varying degrees of self-governance in North America. When they said, "We the People," they did not create ex nihilo.

The founders began not with nothing but with a reality, a given. The given reality, the people, was not simply something they were stuck with; it was a gift, a very imperfect gift with which they struggled. People in some 550 towns in New England had engaged in civil self-governance, and many had acquired experience in the direction of church bodies in that region and elsewhere in the nation-to-be. The perceived element of gift differed in the two settings, ecclesiastical and civil. Religious people recognized God as the giver of gifts, including the gift of their common life as a people and their duties as citizens. Others would not use biblical language, but the element of gift was there in civil discourse. They began with the given of their life together as citizens, which they respected by engaging in public deliberations, complying with the law, and serving variously their neighbors and the public good. Either way, whether as members of civil or ecclesiastical bodies, people were used to the rough carpentry of legislating, the business of executing and enforcing laws, and the solemn task of judging disputes among themselves. Together these functions constituted the public life of a people, and these activities constituted what John Adams and others at the time called their "public happiness," a phrase that sounds odd to modern ears.

Neither the word "people" nor the phrase "public happiness" was a fiction. We are so used to associating happiness with private happiness today that we can miss the animating principle of the American Revolution and the Constitution that followed. When Samuel Adams and others affirmed the principle of "no taxation without representation," the complaint focused on the last, not the first, part of the slogan. (The taxes on tea against which Adams and others protested were miniscule. Indeed, the British made tea available more cheaply with the tax than without it.) The tea tax did not put a crimp on their *private* happiness by reducing their purses. They objected instead to being without representation. They were not willing to pay taxes imposed by the British House of Commons because they were not represented there. That state of affairs deprived them of their *public* happiness, their right to be seen and heard, to make themselves understood in public forum and in political commerce with their fellows. Without the freedom to live and act in concert with others, the merely private life, as variants of the word itself suggest, reflects the diminished life: "privative," "deprived"—impoverished.

The political philosopher Hannah Arendt argued that the day when the great phrase "life, liberty, and the pursuit of happiness" came to mean exclusively "private happiness" marked a great misfortune for the Republic.[12] From that day forward, we began to treat the public realm as a necessary evil, as though it serves merely private ends. We did not expect to enjoy happiness in the public domain. As if to illustrate Arendt's insight, publicists on the political right in 2009 organized a series of "tea parties" on income tax day, April 15, 2009, to link their protest against taxes with the revolutionary protest. The link was false. Leaders of the modern right oppose taxes because they see them as diminishing their purse, their private happiness. This complaint hardly resembles the revolutionary protest, which was not against taxes but against taxation without representation. To be without representation denies citizens their public happiness, their right to participate in the public domain. In 2008, however, the right had the power to participate as volubly as they wished in elections. They lost. Fortunately, the founders sought to affirm the domain of public happiness not only by resisting British authority but by relocating authority where their own exercise of it, in cameo, convinced them it belonged—in "We the People." The Americans already had in place, locally and incipiently and imperfectly, the culture and institutions that would help shape the society to come.[13]

THE BIBLICAL BACKGROUND

The scriptures of Israel supply the deep religious background for the two elements of reality and project that surface in the founding of the United States. The great narrative events of Exodus and Mount Sinai held together this doubleness. The event of the Exodus marked the original gift of deliverance that settled into the being and bowels, the imagination and will of the Israelites, altering their identity. The event of Mount Sinai specified the task, the promised discipline, undertaken by the people in response to the gift. The promise ratifies, rather than creates out of nothing, this alteration of identity. Gift and task together constitute the calling: God's covenant with the people and the people's covenant with God.

The German language draws together more clearly than English the concepts of gift and task with the words "*Gabe*" and "*Aufgabe.*" The repetition of the same syllable in both words conveys the sense that the task flows from the gift. A gift propels toward a task. A charge moves toward a discharge. The Israelites purportedly lived within the sound of gift and task.

The covenantal promise recognizes the gift; and the contents of the promise specify the task. The biblical covenant does not arise from the purely natural biological tie of a child to its parent projected into the relations of a subject to a king or queen. Down that road lie organic, hierarchical governments. Covenantally understood, a government emerges rather from a promise, an agreement, arising from what the community recognizes and receives as a gift—its own being, however imperfect, as a community. The exodus precedes Mount Sinai just as the gifts of courtship precede a marriage vow. Inevitably, the prophets of Israel and the Apostle Paul employed the metaphor of marriage to express the promissory bond between God and the people. The conviction of undeserved grace precedes the answering vow and commitment.

The interpretation of the biblical covenant proposed here differs from the view of the encyclopedist on covenantal theory, Daniel J. Elazar.[14] In my judgment Elazar wrongly eliminated the ingredient of gift in his account of the biblical covenant. He highlighted instead a process of negotiation and bargaining. Christians, he believed, held to the notion of God's unilateral act of grace, which has led them eventually and unfortunately away from the concept of a covenant (reached through bargaining) toward an organic, hierarchical understanding of church and government in the Catholic and Orthodox churches.[15] Elazar's view forced him to overlook the degree to which much of the negotiating, bargaining, and promising in the Torah answers to a reality experienced as a gift, perduringly and unassailably itself. The prophets of Israel—especially Hosea and Ezekiel—were very clearheaded about the giftedness of the gift. The exodus, the event of deliverance, did not reward Israel for a prior virtue or merit. God chose Israel and bestowed upon the people the land of promise not because Israel was talented and outperformed all other nations on her SATs.[16] Elazar's criticism of the doctrine of grace also flew in the face of the historical fact that the Puritans, more than almost all other Christians, affirmed the powerfulness of God's grace and yet hardly embraced an organic, hierarchical understanding of civil and religious government. Indeed, without much hesitation the Puritans tossed kings out of office, and worse.

Taken together, the two aspects of covenant, gift and task, alter the being of the covenanted people (God marks the Jews forever; Ex 24:8, 28:38) so that fidelity to the covenant defines their subsequent life. The people accept an inclusive set of ritual and moral obligations by which they will live. The Torah serves as Israel's constitution, as it were.[17] Its narrative literature (*agada*) recounts the defining gift; and its commands (*halacha*) are both specific enough to make the duties of Israel concrete (e.g., laws governing protection of the weak and showing hospitality to strangers) yet summary and comprehensive enough to require a fidelity beyond the details of a contract. Similarly the Declaration of Independence and the preamble to the Constitution supply the basic narrative (the *agada*) that justifies the action. The Constitution, following the preamble, supplies the structure (the *halacha*) for the society in the making. However, to say that covenantal thinking solely shaped the structure and the animating spirit of the Constitution overstates the case.[18] Other strands of thought in the Enlightenment influenced the founders in substance, not merely in rhetoric. But a covenantal sense of the human condition helps supply the cultural soil out of which the national identity emerges and from which it irregularly draws its life.

Contracts and covenants, materially considered, appear to be first cousins: Both include an agreement and an exchange between parties. But in spirit and sensibility, contracts and covenants differ markedly. Contracts are external; covenants are internal to the parties involved. People sign contracts to discharge them expediently. Contracts are limited and time-bound—whether they pertain to building a house or fixing a leaky roof. In contrast a covenant—such as the covenants of religious people before God or covenants of friendship (Jonathan and David), marriage (cited by the prophets to describe Israel's relation to God), and eventually the Constitution of the United States—ratifies and extends into the future an alteration of identity toward which the original exchange of gifts moves. Contracts operate at the level of buying and selling; covenants augment at the deeper level of giving and receiving. The first level can (and sometimes does) shift into the second when a donative element begins to define the relationship. A contract moves into a covenant when a gratuitous, growing edge to the relation begins to alter identity. Abraham Lincoln recognized the difference between a contract and a covenant when he referred to the original union as a "regular marriage."[19] The founders would not have been as comfortable as President Lincoln in using the biblical metaphor of marriage to describe their work, but a covenantal sensibility informed the union he recognized and sought to preserve.

A word of caution is appropriate here about the profound but morally dangerous alteration of identity that a covenant can effect. As often used today, covenants describe a deep and determined bond between parties, formed to exclude outsiders. Real estate, country club, and church covenants have been formed to wall off a group of people from the intrusions of aliens. Such covenants are designed to keep others from buying their way in. They fly below rather than above the moral level of contracts. Scripture deals with this issue of exclusion.

The very event that sets the people of Israel apart from their neighbors places the stranger within the compass of Israel's duties. "When a stranger sojourns with you in your land, you shall not do him wrong. The stranger who sojourns with you shall be as the native among you; and you shall love him as yourself, for you were strangers in the land of Egypt; I am the Lord your God" (Lv 19:33–34). The question of opening to the stranger tests the depth and breadth of both Israel's covenant and the American covenant to this day.

Taken seriously, the two sides to a covenant—gift and task—define the self as steward rather than owner. We operate daily in the contractual arena of owning, buying, and selling, but that arena does not in itself exhibit the depth and breadth of the world we inhabit as stewards, selves beholden in all we undertake. In the most intimate of areas, who can think of themselves as owners? Who can own his or her child or mate? In those relations, we are stewards at most and at our best—and stewards as well in our rising, studying, working, buying and selling, voting, and governing. "What have you that you did not receive? If then you received it, why do you boast, as if it were not a gift?" (1 Cor 4:7).

THE CALVINIST LEGACY

The biblical understanding of public life was carried forward religiously into the United States via John Calvin and the Puritans. Calvin, more than any other Reformation leader, recognized the importance of government itself as a gift and a task. Toward the end of his four books titled *Institutes of the Christian Religion*, Calvin defended the institution of government against sectarians on the left wing of the Reformation who wanted to eliminate or withdraw from civil government by condemning it as "the damned ruling over the damned." He also rejected the view of those who grudgingly tolerated government as a necessary evil. Far from ranking it as an evil, Calvin recognized government as a gift, as fundamental to human well-being as the gifts of bread and water, light and air: "It is perfect barbarism to think of exterminating it [civil government], its use among men being not less than bread and water, light and air, while its dignity is much more excellent." The value of government lies not only in its use for survival "to enable men to breathe, eat, drink, and be warmed (though it certainly includes all of these . . .)" but also in its further aid in human flourishing. Government can support those further goods and practices hospitable both to religion (Thomas Jefferson would not weigh in on that subject for another two hundred years) and to "humanity among men."[20]

At the same time, Calvin recognized government, both ecclesiastical and civil, as a task. More than Luther, Calvin supplied Protestants in the new world with a serious major alternative to the political vision of Thomas Aquinas. Luther's sense of the element of gift in human life was too restricted to undertake the task of restructuring civil government. God's grace touched the inner life of men and women with forgiveness but left the outer world of political structures relatively untouched. Calvin moved beyond the inherent conservatism of the Lutheran position on government. He recognized the further reach of the covenant of grace beyond forgiveness toward the reordering and energizing of life, inner and outer, ecclesiastical and civil.

However, the road to transformation should not lead to theocracy. The ecclesiastical and civil orders differ from one another. Church order should not be confused with the kingdom of God, and it should not displace civil order. The offices of magistrate and minister are distinct. By the same token Calvin did not fuse democracy with the kingdom of God, as though democracy were an inherently superior form of government that a grateful world would eventually receive through the generosity of the Americans.

While God supplies the gift and call for order, the ways in which humans fittingly respond to the gift belong in part to human art. (Of the three basic forms of government—monarchical, aristocratic, and democratic—Calvin seemed to prefer some mix of the latter two.) However, absolutizing any form of government leaves too little room for differing circumstances of time and place and for criticism and improvement in performance.

In his single-volume tour de force on Western political thought, the political theorist Sheldon Wolin identified Calvin as having engaged in nothing less than the "political education of Protestantism."[21] The church is not a formless religious fellowship. While the ecclesiastical and political orders differ, they also resemble one another. Both are vertebrate. They call for structure; they reflect the importance of law in giving form to the ways in which people live. That emphasis on the importance of structure would carry forward much later on the American scene with a concern for the basic external form and design of the US Constitution.

However, Calvin also recognized the importance of a society's animating spirit to its flourishing. This second emphasis would have its counterpart on the American scene in the eventual concern for the inward dynamics of a covenant that the design of a government alone does not supply. A lawyer himself, Calvin saw that a kind of perverse antinomianism of the law can inspirit the members of a purely legalistic society. Clients and their litigators can exploit the law to provide themselves with a blue line that lets them know what they can maximally get away with. Thus, while emphasizing the importance of a legal system in opposing the sectarians (who believed that resort to the civil law was unchristian), Calvin also criticized a litigious spirit that exploits the law only to serve a runaway malice and appetite: "For there are many who boil with rage for litigation, that they can never be quiet with themselves unless they are fighting with others. Lawsuits they prosecute with the bitterness of deadly hatred, and with an insane eagerness to hurt and revenge, and they persist in them with implacable obstinacy, even to the ruin of their adversary. Meanwhile, that they may be thought to do nothing but what is legal, they use this pretext of judicial proceedings as defense of their perverse conduct."[22]

Inveighing against a "madness for litigation," Calvin proposed a different spirit and sensibility to sustain public life. This spirit undercuts the sense of oneself as an affronted owner in life and redefines the self as the steward of gifts received. In rhetoric that resembles the repetitions found in a liturgy, Calvin affirmed that we are not our own; we are God's.[23] The language is avowedly religious. Calvin appealed to the Holy Spirit, not to the later Enlightenment notion of public-spiritedness. However, the spring of action in both settings calls for sacrifice directed to the common good: "The legitimate use of our gifts is a kind and liberal communication of them with others."[24]

Calvin summarized the set of virtues, so dedicated and disciplined, with the phrase "self-denial." It differs from a Stoic rejection of the passions that would turn a human into a stone (Calvin's image).[25] Neither Calvin nor the later Puritans were on the hunt for a kind of theological Agent Orange that withers the passions of fear and desire. Self-denial does not oppose natural fear, anxiety, and anger; it would contain them.[26] Such self-discipline would free the self to move confidently and steadily in public terrain to serve the common good. Traces of that Calvinist wisdom surfaced 350 years later in George Kennan's advice to the United States on foreign policy. To contain threats to its life, the nation needed first to contain its own fears and angers.

The ethic of self-denial also does not oppose the natural human desires for the necessities of life and for goods beyond the necessities that bring enjoyment and delight. It does, however, oppose and would curb "a frenzied desire, an infinite eagerness, to pursue wealth and honour, intrigue for power, accumulate riches, and collect all those frivolities which seem conducive to luxury and splendor."[27] A trace of that discipline appeared later in John Maynard Keynes's countercyclical economic policies. A society should tax in good times to contain the excesses and inequities in wealth that throw an economy out of balance and into a recession and depression; and it should invest in bad times to help pull a society out of its fears and distrust. Both frenzied desire and runaway fear undercut the capacity of a people to serve their common good and affirm their identity in the declaration "We the People."

6

FORMING A MORE PERFECT UNION

The Task

The previous chapter concentrated on the element of gift in national identity—"We the People." This chapter attends to the task—
forming "a more perfect Union." That purpose heads the list of common aims in the preamble. The further aims of the people include establishing justice and insuring domestic tranquility, providing for the
common defense, promoting the general welfare, and securing the
several "Blessings of Liberty to ourselves and our Posterity." The decision to start with the purpose of forming a more perfect union does
not of itself establish a hierarchical ordering of aims. However, beginning with that purpose boldly distinguishes the founders' intention
from the time-bound horizon of a contract that commits discrete
parties to a series of tasks which, once accomplished, release the sig-
natories to go their separate ways. The further specified aims have
their own independent validity, but they also help point participants
toward a deepening of their covenantal bond with one another.

THE OUTER COVENANT

The preamble to the Constitution supplies the main purposes that
the outer covenant, the body of the Constitution, facilitates and
serves—not yet perfectly, but better than the Articles of Confederation. These purposes help supply a standard by which the structure
and substance of the Constitution might subsequently be measured

and improved, as elected representatives and officers go about the people's business.

TO PROVIDE FOR THE COMMON DEFENSE AND TO INSURE DOMESTIC TRANQUILITY

The people's covenant with themselves surely needed to equip the nation to address negative threats to its life. The people faced the threat of invasion from abroad, possible tyranny from within, and the chronic frustrations of anarchy, both in pressing a war to victory and in holding the country together under the weak Continental Congress. The nation clearly needed to "provide for the common defense" and to "insure domestic tranquility." Otherwise the country could not ensure its survival.

The Articles of Confederation, in striking contrast to the Constitution, did not include in the statement of purpose the aim of providing for the common defense. Under the Articles each state, not the federal government, would provide for its own defense. This omission fit in with the Articles' opening explanation that, in establishing a permanent federal government, each state was "acting in its sovereign and independent character." In contrast, the Constitution locates final sovereignty in the people, not conceiving the nation as an aggregate of individual sovereign states. Fittingly, providing for the common defense belonged among the set of purposes with which the people charged the federal government in forming a more perfect union.

TO ESTABLISH JUSTICE

It should be noted that the preamble places the aims of domestic tranquility and defense in a larger portfolio of purposes, beginning with justice. In their understanding of justice the founders were indeed men of property. They did not specify in the document the full range of classical concerns in matters of justice. The body of the document emphasizes only the first two of the three types of justice that the classical Catholic tradition had elaborated: commutative, legal, and distributive (or ministering) justice.

Commutative justice refers to the fair treatment of parties in their contractual exchanges with one another and is enforceable by the government. The Constitution prepares the way for such enforcement. (However, it removes entirely from view blacks, who as slaves did not qualify as parties to a contract; and it leaves untouched the issue of large inequalities in the relative power of parties entering into contracts.) *Legal* justice refers to those duties that parts of the whole owe to the whole, articulated in the laws of the government. The constitutional emphasis on this second form of justice helped earn Americans the general reputation for being law abiding. Americans embraced a government of laws, not of men. Finally, *distributive* (or ministering) justice refers more expansively to what the whole, acting through its government and other centers of power, owes to its parts in addressing the rights and needs of citizens and in supporting their access to common and high goods.

The body of the Constitution does not develop this third aspect of justice, distributive justice, at the federal level. However, distributive justice lies there in the preamble as an unrealized ideal, later specified and variously advanced in the Bill of Rights and in the amendments on civil rights (thirteenth and fifteenth), the income tax (sixteenth), women's voting rights (nineteenth), and the ban on the poll tax (twenty-fourth). The aim of establishing justice sits there in the preamble along with the aim of promoting the general welfare, a goal with which distributive justice overlaps. The task of promoting the general welfare implies that government will not limit its role solely to the negative function of protecting against the evils of foreign invasion, theft, mayhem, and murder. Government also has a positive role—to promote the general welfare. There is a productive and a distributive side to advancing the general welfare. In his campaign for ratification James Madison cited "improvements" in serving the general welfare, which we would list among the goods of infrastructure today—roads, canals, aids to travel, interior navigation, and the like (*Federalist Papers*, no. 14). The government in the making was intended to serve not only the nation's being but its well-being, not only its existence but its developed existence, not only its survival but its flourishing. The recognition of this positive, productive service to welfare also carries with it a ministerial responsibility for providing citizens with fair access to common and high goods, the duty of distributive justice. The recognition of these positive functions should eventually have the salutary effect of keeping the government more balanced, less anxious, and therefore—contrary to current rhetoric—more proportional in its size. A nation that tends to its flourishing and well-being, as well as its being, may be more confident and less rattled by the inevitable passing threats to its survival.

Free marketers today tend to dismiss the preamble's stated national purpose of promoting the general welfare as if the phrase were mere boilerplate or a throwaway line. However, the phrase is notably missing in the prior Articles of Confederation as a national mission but quite deliberately placed in the preamble to the Constitution. Promoting the general welfare appears to be one of the stated purposes of the people in their effort to form a more perfect union, not simply an afterthought. It seems reasonable to take this aim seriously and honor it as a goal by which legislation should be measured and the workings of the Constitution itself, through amendment, should be further perfected.

The preamble closes with the task of securing the "blessings of liberty," which the people quickly specified in a bill of rights, the first order of business in amending the Constitution. The blessings of liberty—most notably the freedoms of religion, speech, press, and peaceable assembly and the right of a trial by jury—are not private liberties but civil liberties. They do not simply carve out a little cave where each individual is on his or her own. They clear a space for the deliberations of the people as they freely debate, consider, and pursue questions of justice and the common good, as they affirm the community they are while pointing toward a community still in the making.

The founders sensibly linked freedom of religion with the freedoms of speech, press, and assembly because religion is not simply a matter of what one does in one's private hours. It is part of the deliberative underpinnings of a republic. The liberty for which the Bill of Rights seeks to clear a space is an active, participatory, civil liberty. A merely private liberty would not long survive unless, in the active uses of their liberty, the American people sustained a readiness to serve the common good. Justice Stephen Breyer described such active, participatory liberty as the basic thrust of the Constitution.[1] He described active liberty as the context for that text, the Word within the words of that document. It justifies the explicit extension of those liberties to all people across the Thirteenth and Fourteenth Amendments, and it animated in the twentieth century some of the major decisions of the Court.

Several contending views of freedom figure in debates about liberty in legislative halls, in the courts, and in the seminar rooms of historians. The tradition distinguishes between negative and positive liberty. Negative liberty refers to a freedom *from* intrusions by others, especially the government. Positive liberty emphasizes a freedom *to;* it emphasizes the goal of self-mastery in the uses of one's negative liberty. Still others would add a freedom *for.* In my judgment the Bill of Rights pushes beyond a negative liberty (freedom *from* the British) toward a positive liberty (a freedom *toward* the self-governance of the nation) and moves still further toward a freedom *for others.*

Those who take seriously a freedom *for* would recognize (as the liberal does) that negative freedom conditions the exercise of positive freedom. Crippling intervention into the lives of others inhibits both self-mastery and self-sacrifice. But at the same time, negative liberty is not itself preconditionless. A refusal to impose on others does not by itself create a society that lives by that ideal. Only insofar as men and women live by the positive warrants of a freedom to and a freedom for do they shape a culture that gives space and place to the negative liberty of others. It is not enough to leave others alone to satisfy the demands of negative liberty. It may be necessary to be *for* them and indeed to sacrifice for them for their negative liberty to flourish.

Politically, a freedom for others articulates those overriding goals that citizens, with imperfect practice in being "We the People," pursue as they move toward a more perfect union. The goals of justice, domestic tranquility, common defense, general welfare, and the blessings of liberty constitute the original covenant, the moral vector of the nation.[2]

THE CONSTITUTIONAL STRUCTURE

The body of the Constitution following the preamble deals with the structure of government to be ordained and established. The proposed structure articulates a legislative, executive, and judicial power beyond the capabilities of the Continental Congress. This articulation of power should not be construed, in the fashion of social contract theory, as a forfeit. This articulation would increase the nation's power not only to deal with the negative threats of tyranny and anarchy but also to serve the positive ends of justice and the general welfare. It augments rather than forfeits power, creating what Alexander Hamilton called a more energetic and efficient government (*Federalist Papers,* nos. 70, 71).

But this increase in power needs to operate within a framework of order in an imperfect world. Getting rid of the British did not get rid of sin, either in the people or in their government. Self-interest would continue to drive people and their leaders. Legislators, magistrates, and judges do not, by virtue of their office, escape from the human condition. As Madison famously put it, "you must first enable the government to control the governed; and in the next place oblige it to control itself." (*Federalist Papers,* no. 51).

To accomplish that purpose Madison and his colleagues, drawing on the ideas of the Baron de Montesquieu, advocated the mechanism of checks and balances that, far from curtailing self-interest, would partly rely on its omnipresent power to blunt its negative effects. A separation of powers between the legislative, executive, and judicial branches of government and the division of powers between local, state, and national authorities would pit ambition against ambition so that no individual, faction, or majority could dominate all others. Through the device of countervailing powers the framers sought to solve the problem of governance that human nature posed (what Madison called the "defect of better motives" in the *Federalist Papers,* nos. 51, 10). A system of checks and balances slyly mimics nature itself. The device of pitting ambition against ambition reiterates in political structures the natural phenomenon of force and counterforce. The mechanism of the Constitution would keep the country from tearing itself to pieces without demanding much virtue from its citizens or leaders.

Daniel J. Elazar likened—somewhat too ingeniously in my judgment—the constitutional device of checks and balances to the critical role of the prophets in standing up to the kings in ancient Israel.[3] Elazar's analogy is a stretch. The extramural powers exercised by a prophet differ from the built-in checks and balances designed by Madison and colleagues. The prophets gave voice to the voiceless, whose interests the powerful had drowned out, whereas the founders of the Constitution sought to check and balance competing interests within the system. The more apt analogy to the prophetic role might be the Bill of Rights, however, in its full exercise. At least potentially the freedoms of religion, speech, and press point toward an active liberty that might speak truth to power. Otherwise the country suffers great loss when religious leaders, lawyers, accountants, journalists, and teachers are uncritically influenced by the powers that feed them. The United States needs its independent prophets working both inside and outside the walls of government and the corporations if these huge complexes of power are to serve the country better.

If interpretation were to stop at this point, relying solely on *Federalist Papers* 10 and 51, the American Mount Sinai would seem to have solved—wholly through the mechanism of checks and balances—the political problem that a fallen human nature poses. The Constitution offers a procedural republic that would harness the energies of self-interest, while blunting the negative effects of a human nature untransformed. In this interpretation Madison and other federalists were secular heirs of the Reformation tradition. They were not romantics about people or idealists about human nature, nor were they religiously naive. Sufficiently practiced in the politics of 1776 to 1787, they wrestled with the reality of what theologians call the sinfulness of humankind and what the founders recognized as the destructive power of uncurbed self-interest in human affairs.

However, as the historian William Lee Miller put it in his fine volume on Madison, the federalists were "calmly realistic" rather than "fiercely pessimistic" about human nature.[4] They did not propose to take the country in the direction of Lutheran conservatism in politics. Nor did they opt for a Machiavellian cynicism that would simply coach ambitious leaders in how to survive in a treacherous sea of self-interested people.[5] Nor for that matter were the federalists as pessimistic about people as the anti-federalists, who were afraid to venture beyond the safety of their own states for fear that a national government would swamp them with populist movements originating elsewhere.[6]

Madison and colleagues applied their realism about human nature for progressive rather than conservative purposes. They "interpreted the limitations of humankind neither to support the order imposed by powers that be nor to dismiss all efforts at beneficent change." In fact, like John Calvin, Madison recognized the importance of structure in sustaining changes and proposed, as Miller phrased it, "an immense alteration in the structure of the human lot."[7]

These alterations did not claim to create a perfect union—simply a "more perfect" union. More perfect than what? More perfect than the Articles of Confederation then in force. The Articles lacked the structure to let people deal more confidently with the threats the several states faced, either separately or in their ineffectual alliance. Madison's project was melioristic rather than utopian. Clearly, a union that is simply better than it was also needs to provide the means for its continuing improvement. The Articles of Confederation had effectively ruled out the possibility of their improvement by demanding that the states reach unanimous agreement in making any change whatsoever. The Constitution at least opened the door—from a later vantage point, perhaps much too cautiously—to its continuing self-improvement through amendment.

THE INNER COVENANT: PUBLIC CULTURE

The success of constitutional government does not rest solely on the ingenuity of the federalists in designing a self-improving mechanism and structure to keep inveterately self-interested people working together in spite of themselves. The nation's success also depends on a public culture that grounds those structures and shapes the inner covenant. Something more than self-interest needs to figure in the mix of motives that supports a durable politics. This other half of the mix of motives shows up during the constitutional period in *Federalist Papers* 14 and 55, not in the more widely read 10 and 51. In *Federalist Paper* 14, the unsentimental Madison wrote of the "many cords of affection" that knit together the American family. At the close of *Federalist Paper* 55, he tried to look at human nature, steady and whole, spelling out its implications for politics:

> As there is a degree of depravity in humankind which requires a certain degree of circumspection and distrust, so there are

other qualities in human nature which justify a certain portion of esteem and confidence. Republican government presupposes the existence of these qualities in a higher degree than in any other form. Were the pictures formed by the political jealousies of some among us faithful likenesses of the human character, the inference would be that there is not sufficient virtue among men for self-government; and that nothing less than the chains of despotism can restrain them from destroying and devouring one another.

In 1788 Madison firmly wrote, "To suppose that any form of government will secure liberty without any virtue in the people, is a chimerical idea."[8]

The earlier revolutionaries had agreed. "Public virtue" ranked second to liberty as the term most often invoked at the time of the Revolution.[9] The virtue entailed a readiness to sacrifice self-interest to the common good. Why public virtue? Instrumentally the revolutionaries recognized the need for self-sacrifice in winning the war of independence—the risks and sacrifices of not only soldiers but also leaders who placed themselves at risk by signing the Declaration of Independence. The revolutionaries also recognized that, long after the urgencies of war abated, the country would need public virtue in its citizens to sustain the nation's character as a republic, a res publica.

The revolutionaries had not invented the idea of public virtue. They drew on earlier, more communitarian layers in American culture, civic as well as religious, that nourished public life. Most immediately they drew on the thought of Montesquieu, who had argued that a republic, whether democratic or aristocratic, requires not only a constitutional structure to supply it with order but an *arche* (that is, an animating principle to drive it).[10] Governments need a fundamental spring of action to draw people out of their privacy into the public realm. Whereas despots rely on fear and monarchs on the aspiration to excellence to set their respective societies in motion, a democratic republic must rely on civic virtue to sustain the public realm. The structure of a republic needs to be inspirited by some readiness in its citizens to sacrifice for the common good.

Public virtue does not grow without cultivation. The Constitution —a piece of paper alone—would not suffice to protect the nation against the corrosion of self-interest. The country would need the active engagement of two institutions in forming the American character: religious institutions and educational institutions. So John Adams remarked after the completion of the document.

Educational institutions have played an obvious role in cultivating the American Republic. Citizens need some verbal facility to exercise their civil rights under the First Amendment and to participate fully in public affairs. Schools have also supplied the basic verbal and mathematical skills, apart from which citizens and recently arrived immigrants cannot take full advantage of the work life that an expanding economy offers. Socially and culturally, the schools have also helped draw children out of the privacy of the home into public spaces—the classroom, the library, the playground and athletic fields—where they learn how to deal with strangers on the long road to becoming citizens. Sooner or later, overtaxed schools become the sites where most of the accumulating problems in a democracy surface and test public virtue.

The role of religious institutions in forming the American character, at the time of Adams's statement, reflected partly, not exclusively, the double influence of the Calvinist tradition in the country. Clearly Calvin (and the Puritan preachers following him in the New World) emphasized the importance of structures, intellectual, ecclesiastical, and civil. This high regard for structure led to 150 years of experience in drawing up compacts that bear on governance and helped inspire civic pride in being a government of laws, not men. At the same time, Calvin had emphasized the importance of an animating spirit—holy rather than perverse—in sustaining the inward covenant and common life. In effect the religious life included two sides: the mind illumined and the heart warmed. This Calvinism crossed the Atlantic with the Puritans.

THE PURITAN TRANSPLANT

At length, in the middle of the eighteenth century, the Puritans in the United States split into two groups: the "Old Lights" and the

"New Lights." The Old Lights emphasized theological reasoning and the delivery of orthodox sermons that satisfied without disturbing the expectations of the mind. They also maintained good order and structure in the churches and, as pastors and lay people, transmitted the received tradition. However, opponents questioned whether the tradition could be truly received if it was *pro forma*—that is, if it lacked Calvin's powerful conviction that a true knowledge of God prompts a transforming self-knowledge that enlivens the innermost springs of action.

Thus, in reaction to a tradition drying up, the New Lights of the Great Awakening of the 1730s and 1740s celebrated the power of the Holy Spirit, as the Spirit quickened the heart and stirred even the bodies of those who came alive. Believers—born again—were no longer the half-hearted recipients of a distanced tradition. Their "awakenings" rattled ecclesiastical and liturgical structures. They pared down congregations (and their leaders) to those members who could pass the raised bar in religious fervor. And their itinerant charismatic preachers tended to unravel local authority as they traveled across borders and transcended ordinary ecclesiastical structures and controls.

The towering Jonathan Edwards, from 1734 onward, figured as a leader, preacher, and historian, but also as a critic of the Great Awakening. Like Calvin he wanted to honor both structure and spirit and, correlatively, both the mind and the heart in the religious covenant. He famously balanced the role of reason and religious experience in the apprehension of God: "Where there is a kind of light without heat, a head stored with notions and speculations, with a cold and unaffected heart, there can be nothing divine in that light." Yet at the same time, "where there is heat without light there can be nothing divine or heavenly in that heart."[11] While Edwards and Calvin affirmed both the mind and the heart in the religious life, each theologian began at the opposite location in covering the whole. Calvin began with the mind's knowledge of God, and Edwards unapologetically began with the religious affections: "All will allow that true virtue and holiness has its seat chiefly in the heart rather than the head."[12] Edwards's starting point in the religious affections, though not his Calvinist theology, eventually carried forward variously in successive waves of revival in Protestant America, and of course it appears in the agendas of large denominations—Baptist, Methodist, Nazarene, Pentecostal, and many others—to this day. Inner feeling more than outer form tends to matter the most in the religious life.

More important for the purposes of this discussion, the First Great Awakening (about 1735 to 1750) prepared the way for three features of the political landscape ahead. First, the evangelical movement transcended civil and ecclesiastical boundaries and thereby prepared the way for a sense of national feeling. Prior experience in civil and church government gave leaders considerable practice in being a people and acting on behalf of a people *locally*, but the first great revival crossed borders. It was interdenominational and often intercolonial in impact. The great missionary George Whitefield preached to the multitudes from Georgia to New England across theological and ecclesiastical boundaries. Such itinerant preachers helped create and relied on a bond of fellowship that transcended differences in doctrine and polity. Common religious experience helped supply a background that kept the later proclamation "We the People" from seeming a stretch.

Second, common religious feeling also intensified a moral resolution to sacrifice self-interest to the common good, a disposition that harmonized with the later Republican call for public virtue. In a sermon preached before John Hancock in 1780, Samuel Cooper declared, "Virtue is the spirit of a Republic; for where all power is derived from the people, all depends on their good disposition."[13] Benjamin Rush welcomed Christian support for such Republican views. Reason "produces, it is true, great and popular truths, but it affords *motives* too weak to induce mankind to act agreeably to them. Christianity unfolds the same truths and accompanies them with *motives*, agreeable, powerful, and irresistible."[14] The Calvinist preacher Nathaniel Niles challenged the proposition that reason unfolds the same truth as scripture. The Lockean account of rational origins, based on antecedent self-interest, offers little resource for sustaining the disposition of public virtue. Niles said, "If 'government is first founded on private interest, it cannot be reasonably expected that the superstructure will stand.'"[15] In the course of time the question as to just what kind of virtue and superstructure truly endures changed. As the historian Alan Heimert wryly observed, the subject for sermons increasingly was not "the perseverance of the saints, but of patriots."[16]

A third political impact of the Great Awakening traces back partly to Edwards's conviction that the stirrings of the Spirit supply evidence that something new is aborning in America. God does not begin his "work where there is some good growth already, but in a wilderness, where nothing grows, and nothing is to be seen. . . . What is now seen in America and especially in New England, may prove to be the dawn of that glorious day . . . God intends it as the beginning or forerunner of something vastly great."[17] Edwards helped articulate a sense of America's unique vocation and destiny that found its way eventually into the second, somewhat sonorous, phrase embossed on the great seal of the United States—*novus ordo seclorum*, a "new order of the ages." America represents a break with the past and will usher in a new order of the ages.

Down the road of this American exceptionalism lies the temptation to American imperialism. Along that road Presidents Andrew Jackson, James Polk, and Theodore Roosevelt traveled. Still later, Woodrow Wilson's mission to make the world safe for democracy darkened and hardened into the neoconservative project to convert the republic into a unipolar empire. Edwards had theological resources for criticizing a patriotism that bottles up in idolatry. Edwards defined true virtue as benevolence to being in general, a spaciousness that hardly narrows down to a nation's resolve to dominate all beings.

What does it mean to usher in a "new order of the ages"? A calling to bear witness to such an order differs from a compulsion to impose it on others. John Winthrop's earlier biblical metaphor of a city built on a hill suggests a city that serves as a beacon to others, not a command center to which the world must defer. The latter view of destiny as command produces a double distortion. A nation so conceived leaves no place and space either for other nations or for its own self-criticism. It suppresses the Psalmist's sober sense of our common political condition: "Let the nations know that they are only human" (Ps 9:20).

Alexis de Tocqueville still saw evidences of a more temperate call for patriotism and public spiritedness in the 1840s, when he characterized the Americans as a "people ready to make small sacrifices." The phrase is apt. Maybe we are not a nation of great heroes, in the fashion of a Joan of Arc or a Gandhi, but we are a nation capable of small sacrifices, for which he reserved in another passage the term "covenant": "a covenant exists . . . between all the citizens of a democracy when they all feel themselves subject to the same weakness and the same dangers; their interests as well as their compassion makes it a rule with them to lend one another assistance when required." The national covenant builds on this imperfect reality of gift and task, both preceding and sustaining it: no single heroic deed, but the countless unrecorded sacrifices that allow citizens eventually to recognize themselves as a people and to act on this recognition.[18]

THE FLAWED COVENANT

No one has diagnosed the deep flaw of the Constitution more acerbically than Barbara Jordan, the Democratic congresswoman from Texas. She remarked that when the founders proclaimed "We the People," they left her out. Worse yet, the founders counted her and her slave ancestors as three-fifths of a person, thereby increasing the relative political weight of the votes of slave masters as the government calculated the number of representatives the slave-holding states would enjoy in Congress and the power those states could wield in the electoral college. The original Constitution included two other provisions on slavery: one establishing 1808 as the date on which the slave trade might possibly (but only possibly) end, and the other concerning the enforced return of runaway slaves to their states and masters of origin. Shrewdly enough, the original document never used the word "slave." It relied on euphemisms— "other persons" or "such persons" or "persons held to service or labor." The resort to euphemisms reflected, at one level, shame over the institution, a recognition that slavery violates nature so deeply that one cannot bear to name it. At the same time, by referring to slaves as "other persons" rather than property, the founders spared the slave-holding states the possible political inconvenience that would fall on them if other states, rich in property (such as horses, carriages, houses, and bushels of corn), should question the validity of counting slaves as more valuable than other kinds of property in the calculus of political power.

The phrase "We the People" also left out Native American populations. "We the People" subjected them to treaties and covenants regularly broken, so much so that the historian Edward Countryman argued that one cannot claim to write a history of the American people, only the histories of the American peoples. The latter task moreover faces the sad barrier that the histories of those left out have been overwhelmed by the destruction of memory and tradition in the schools, where the dominant power has educated them. Further, "We the People" constantly face the temptation to bar the doors to the arrival of immigrant strangers whose skin, accents, and predilections disturb those who do not want to lose the hard-won familiarities and securities of their neighborhoods.

The brilliant phrasing of Jordan's prophetic judgment lays bare the fact that the *content* of the covenant—its provision on slavery— fails a test set by the *source* to which it appeals—"We the People." That source sets a standard of moral coherence by which American life will be measured over and over again. The original story line that begins with "We the People" is not simply a false claim and fiction— it is a myth that possesses, for better or worse, demiurgic power. The story sets up a dynamic. It brings into play what is not yet fully there. You say, "We the People"? How then is it that you go on to stipulate someone is three-fifths of a person and define me out? As a black? As a woman? Such questions will be asked and will launch reform movements and changes in the continuing history of the country. The force of Jordan's question has a power of its own, the import of which not even some of the bards who wrote and told and now retell the story fully realized.

The historian Edmund Morgan, who referred to "We the People" as a fiction (as described in chapter 5 in this book), also recognized the revolutionary import of that fiction.[19] Placing "We the People" at the head of the first sentence in the founding document profoundly repositioned people with respect to sovereignty. Until then people were among the ruled, not themselves rulers. Even in pressing their rights the people could do so only as subjects ruled by others. They had to petition others—the king, a body of aristocrats, or the church—who exercised sovereignty over them. But in the preamble the ruled recognized themselves as rulers. In the Constitution and its ratification they busily engaged in providing themselves with structures by which they bestowed upon some persons among themselves the power to govern in specific ways. This huge shift in sovereignty redefined responsibility.

The people could no longer pass off their responsibility as though they are the ruled. The people became accountable to themselves for the structure and results of that bestowal. The myth of "We the People" is demiurgic in the sense that it began to set in motion facts that produce a world more accurately corresponding to the myth. If people are not simply the ruled but rulers, Jordan and blacks like her in the constitutional era (some 16 percent of Americans at the time) must be counted in. The myth begins to blow back upon itself. It opens the windows and doors to the people. The ruled begin to recognize themselves as rulers and hold themselves and others to it. "The Americans begin to see that government originates not with a king with whom the people make a contract—with some principle of sovereignty antecedent to themselves—but rather solely with a people, who make a covenant with themselves, and a grant of power to government, which is merely their servant."[20]

The bitter ordeals of the Civil War and events beyond eventually tested (and extended) the commitment to what Abraham Lincoln, in his address at Gettysburg, compactly called a government "of the people, by the people, and for the people." The phrase recognizes the people as imperfect source, means, and end. Such a government calls for the virtue of gratitude (a tempered patriotism) in receiving what we already are, the virtue of repentant wisdom in determining our course, and the virtue of hope as we move toward those ends that define our common task.

THE COVENANTAL TASK AHEAD

The unfinished agenda ahead divides into two parts: structural and substantive. The first part would have to deal with structural reforms, constitutional and institutional, that might help the nation make good on its substantive agenda. The second part would deal with those enduring commitments, touching on such matters as security, general welfare, education, health care, jobs, and care of the environment, that will affect the nation's survival and flourishing.

On structural issues some critics have recognized that the founders secured ratification of the Constitution by establishing a Senate that would greatly favor the relative power of sparsely populated states. This imbalance worsened with the subsequent urbanization of the United States, to the general disadvantage of the country on many issues. Unfortunately, however, adopting a constitutional amendment that would rectify the imbalance would itself be difficult to accomplish. Any such amendment would require endorsement by some states ill-disposed to yielding their disproportionate power. Fortunately, other remedies to this structural problem would not require an amendment to the Constitution. They would simply demand changes in recently hardened Senate rules and customs. By exploiting its filibuster power the Senate, from 2008 to 2010, has basically required a supermajority of sixty votes to discuss and pass substantive legislation. Senate rules also have granted a kind of veto power to a single senator that allows him or her to hold up an executive appointment or by that tactic to delay passage of important, unrelated legislation. Such rules and customs blocked important responses in the economic crisis of 2008, but they are not embedded in the Constitution itself. They could be changed. Still other critics worry about the long-range impacts of the Supreme Court decision in *Citizens United v. Federal Elections Commission* on January 21, 2010. In practical effect that decision, in the name of free speech, removes most limits on spending by wealthy corporations, individuals, and unions. It lets them dominate access to the media without obliging them, as the law now stands, to disclose their identity. Such structural issues are serious and surely part of the covenantal agenda ahead, but they are beyond the scope of this book.

Instead, the remainder of this chapter focuses on the substantive aspects of the covenantal agenda ahead. Any elaboration of such commitments in language, relative weight, and scope must recognize the increasing immersion of that discussion in the historical moment, especially as these commitments bear on policy issues. We see through a glass darkly. We do not fully recognize the unbidden in what we have already chosen, the harms exacted by our gains, the prices still to be paid for our omissions, the opportunities unnoticed at our feet. The discernments of the national covenant at any given time are very much those of a people still under way. No particular elaboration of obligations permanently resolves and balances contending claims against it, as people attempt to deal fairly and honorably with competing strands of the covenant that is theirs to tend, mend, and enhance. Enduring obligations only mark out the boundaries. They do not remove the need for the human art of governing on site.

DOMESTIC TRANQUILITY AND COMMON DEFENSE

From the founding to this day, the nation's covenant with itself surely includes domestic tranquility and defense. Police and fire departments play an important role in sustaining domestic order. The armed services and the diplomatic corps protect the country in its dealings with other powers. It would be a species of angelism to deny these roles. However, the Constitution also sets constraints under which the police and military operate when the preamble wisely mentions justice first, before the ends of tranquility and defense, and closes with the blessings of liberty among the ends for which the government came into being. The key challenge the country has faced since World War II and may face yet again is wielding this power on the world scene in a manner faithful to its identity as a republic, not an empire.

THE GENERAL WELFARE

The preamble announces at the very outset that the nation should not, in the fashion of modern libertarians, reduce the government's role solely to the negative functions of protecting against evil but should rather recognize its positive function to promote the general welfare. It will not consign that task to the vagaries of the marketplace alone. The fundamental goods of food, clothing, shelter, and health care are not optional commodities like a tie or a scarf. When the marketplace alone cannot generate or supply these fundamental goods, the government and voluntary communities need to make sure that these goods reach all in need. Without access to these goods people suffer the loss of the further good of community (to be sick without health care reminds the patient, at the worst possible moment, that he or she does not really belong). Promoting the general welfare serves not only participants but the community itself from a constant source of its perishing.

OUR COVENANT WITH THE FUTURE

We make good on our covenant with the future when we ensure that the several goods of general welfare, including the good of education, reach all children. The underfunding of health care and public education for children has been a national shame.

We also covenant with future generations when we fully honor our duties of stewardship to nature. Our rapid depletion of nonrenewable resources, our defiling of air and water, the dwindling of the wilderness and treasured species within it, the destructive impacts of dangerous new processes and products and industrial waste on workers and consumers, and the relentless expenditures of energy that have produced the greenhouse effect and made an enemy of the sun itself—all of these call not only for technological ingenuity but for the discipline of self-regulation, in order to convey an honored earth to generations to come.

OUR COVENANT WITH THE PAST

We seek to honor our covenant with the elderly through Social Security and currently through Medicare and Medicaid and important service organizations. Just as no child should be left behind, so the elderly should not be left stranded, either in their neediness or in their underutilized capacities to serve the needs of others. They should be respected as a public within the public at large, not simply indulged—or feared—as an interest group.

A STEWARDSHIP SOCIETY

As we sustain our multiple obligations to the poor, to children, to the environment, and to the elderly, the country needs to dig more deeply into its grounding in gift than the recent slogan of an ownership society admits. It needs to recover its responsibilities as a stewardship society. As owners we have built up huge trade deficits in sky, sea, and earth that undercut our covenant with the future. At the same time, as stewards we must acknowledge that each fundamental good competes with other basic goods. The wise and efficient use of public funds is not simply an economic but a moral necessity.

AN ETHIC OF PERSONAL RESPONSIBILITY

Such basic goods as education and health care are public goods, in that a huge social investment has created them. We do not adequately honor the social origin of these goods if we think of them as entitlements alone. They call for citizens in active partnership with their education and health care. We need to recover the two sides to citizenship. Late Rome emphasized its entitlements, but Athens emphasized its duties.

OUR COVENANT WITH THE GENERATION IN CHARGE

We need public policies that recognize the contributions of both business investors and workers to the nation's wealth. We fail investors when we pretend that the marketplace is self-corrective, when we deregulate the markets and let assets vaporize into speculative bubbles. Investors and workers ultimately suffer. Workers further suffer through tax policies that have rewarded speculators more than investors and investors more than workers. The government is thereby protractedly partial to a small minority.

A commitment to full employment and to a living wage further broadens and deepens our covenant with the generation in charge. The unemployed do not participate in one of the fundamental goods of a decent society: the dignity of participating in its work life and, through work, meeting obligations to dependents. Meanwhile, the working poor do not fairly enjoy the fruits of their labor when a society flouts the old religious standard of a just wage. Today the working poor must often hold down several jobs to pay the rent and put food on the table. Their families are at risk and their children often lack adult supervision while they supply, through their work, the goods and services upon which the rest of us depend.

OUR COVENANT WITH THE FAMILY

Martin Luther called the family a school for character. The Roman Catholic tradition has concerned itself with the economic underpinnings of the family and its educational and spiritual needs. Memory, nurture, and discipline have characterized the Jewish family across the centuries. The power of the family in still other religious traditions has helped sustain members in their struggles to take hold in a new land. Our national covenant with the family requires relief from economic strains that hamper many in the task of parenting. The national covenant requires strengthening the educational performance of schools and congregations as a practical counterpoint to the teaching authority of the media that dominates the household today. It also means finding some bridges across the pro-life and pro-choice positions on abortion—bridges that, while keeping choice open, would work to keep abortion rare (a formula that dwindles into a slogan unless it includes prenatal and postnatal support for those who would keep their babies). Some see same-sex partnerships and marriage as a threat to the institution of marriage, but policies that encourage fidelity in intimate relations, whether heterosexual or homosexual, seem the better course in serving both them and the institution of marriage.

EXTENDING THE COVENANT TO THE STRANGER

We make good on the several liberties anticipated in the preamble to the Constitution, and on the unfinished story of their extension in the Bill of Rights and in amendments beyond, as we offer the full protection of the law to all persons irrespective of race, gender, sexual orientation, or ethnic origin. All societies are tempted to withdraw from the strange, and America is particularly tempted to do so as an immigrant nation. Periodically, the United States has had to learn how to respect the stranger—through the protection of its legal system, through the tutoring in citizenship that the public school system at its best offers, and through the opening of doors in its houses of worship and service organizations. Such resources help rescue a society from the constant temptation to contract in fear and impoverish itself. No event tests the national covenant more pointedly today than the arrival of undocumented strangers, the subject of the closing chapter of this book.

7

KEEPING COVENANT
WITH IMMIGRANTS AND
UNDOCUMENTED WORKERS

Why close this book with a chapter on the covenant with immigrants and undocumented workers? The answer lies in a comment made in chapter 5. There, the word "covenant" in the biblical setting emphasized an identity deeper than a contractual one. However, a covenantal identity as understood today can be morally dangerous. Devices such as real estate covenants, glass ceilings in the workplace, and tacit church covenants conveniently let a group of people protect themselves from the violation of their space by strangers. Compared with such closed covenants, money can seem positively ecumenical; it opens doors. Inescapably, the arrival of immigrants and undocumented workers in the United States today singularly tests the meaning and probity of the national covenant. Does it simply resemble a real estate covenant writ large or something more?

The general issue of immigration dates back hundreds of years, and the particular issue of undocumented workers has irregularly commanded the national headlines in the twenty-first century. The treatment of the undocumented surfaced dramatically in Iowa during the political campaign of 2008, though it did not rank then at the top of the national agenda. It did not match the continuing war in the Middle East or the bursting of the real estate bubble or the freezing of the financial system or the threatened collapse of the three remaining American automakers, the signature industry of the twentieth century. But the question flared up again with the 2010 passage of a controversial law in the border state of Arizona, the state through which approximately 50 percent of undocumented workers enter the United States. Governor Jan Brewer passed a law (SB 1070) that gives the police broad powers and responsibility to detain anyone suspected of being in the country illegally and that makes the failure of carrying proof of legal status a crime.[1] Not all police chiefs were in favor of this law. Some worried that the new law would distract from other duties and weaken the trust between police and the community that is so important to deal effectively with crime. Other critics saw the new law as an unconstitutional license for racial and ethnic profiling that would in effect presume that Hispanics are guilty, regardless of their immigrant status, until they can prove their innocence by showing their papers. Once again, however, the issue quickly yielded to other headlines, especially the round-the-clock spread of BP oil in the Gulf of Mexico. Still, the problem of immigrant labor continues to trouble and test this immigrant nation.

In July 2007 approximately twelve million people were part of the army of undocumented laborers in the United States—mercenaries on the cheap.[2] They mowed lawns, cared for the elderly, cleared dishes in fast food restaurants, hauled garbage, built tract houses, poured cement, cleaned toilets, changed bedpans, dug potatoes, picked lettuce and tomatoes and avocados, slaughtered turkeys and cattle in our packing houses, and worked multiple jobs, sometimes for ten to seventeen hours a day, without overtime pay or health care benefits. Following the disaster of Hurricane Katrina, undocumented workers along the Gulf Coast delayed showing up at emergency rooms or triage clinics because they feared exposing their illegal status. Generally, illegal immigrants cannot protest against bad working conditions, bullying bosses, or inadequate pay—or no pay—for fear of being turned over to authorities and turned out of the country.

The triggering event in Iowa occurred on May 12, 2008. Federal immigration agents raided a meatpacking plant in the town of Postville and rounded up 389 immigrants, twenty of whom were underage workers, some as young as thirteen years old. Of these immigrants, 297 were convicted on criminal charges for fraud, and most at the time were sentenced to five months in jail after which they would be deported. (Prosecutors could have bypassed the more severe criminal charges by simply deporting them immediately for immigration violations.) "Most of them were from villages in Guatemala who did not understand the criminal charges they were facing or the rights most of them had waived."[3]

After the raid and arrests, wives and children began gathering at St. Bridget's Church (where all but two members of the choir were now gone). Sister Mary McCauley, the parish administrator, sized up the event and left a message asking the out-of-town retired priest to return to Postville, saying, "We need to see a collar here." Mothers who had worked at the plant were not immediately jailed or deported. Authorities put an electronic homing device on women's ankles to keep track of them. They became known as *las personas con brazalete* (the people with a bracelet).[4]

Nothing so dramatic happened immediately to the owners or executives of the packing plant. Some eventually faced criminal charges. However, they could afford to hire good lawyers who spoke in their own tongue. In the meantime, spokespersons for the owners argued that they were the victims of fraud and that, whatever their deficiencies in politeness, they were not in arrears in paying the hourly wage. Still, despite these efforts at damage control, the owners had embarrassed themselves before the public at large and the particular public of customers they served.

What to do about this issue in the nation at large? It is difficult to address politically the issue of immigration and undocumented workers in a country of porous borders, where all citizens except for badly treated Native Americans have an immigrant past. The issue is touchy. Measures seem only to press the boil rather than heal it.

The political split over the issue does not simply reflect a quarrel between Republicans and Democrats. Each party itself is split on the issue. Conservatives among Republicans want to enforce our border to the south with a wall or with electronic devices to protect jobs, stop the drain on taxes, and protect the nation from what they view as a contaminating bilingual identity. They believe that amnesty for twelve million past offenders is unthinkable because it would mock any and all future efforts to secure borders.

Major business interests in the Republican Party have countered that a high, impermeable wall between a rich nation and a poor neighbor would be hard to enforce. Returning twelve million people to their homelands would also damage massively the US economy by raising dramatically the prices paid for food and services. Undocumented workers do the jobs that Americans do not want to do. Further, imposing rules and sanctions on employers would burden those who are often the victims of fraud. It would also put managers in the position of becoming detectives and cops. Meanwhile, lettuce and tomatoes would rot in the fields. Politically, senior members of the Republican Party, from President George W. Bush to Karl Rove and Governor Jeb Bush of Florida, also have recognized that the GOP faces a possible long-term decline into a minority party if it were to lose not only African Americans but Hispanics as potential members.

A split similarly has beset the Democrats on the subject of immigration. Historically, American workers have depended upon the labor unions to help secure livable wages and decent working conditions, but an unstanched flow of desperate immigrants into the country destroys the leverage of workers as a negotiating partner in a free market economy. As for the complaint that Americans will not do these jobs, the unions have countered, pay American workers a fair wage and they will do the work.

Meanwhile, other Democrats have worried about a surge of nativism in the country. They appeal to the liberal past of a democracy that welcomed immigrants who helped build a nation. They recoil at the horrific suffering we would impose on nearly twelve million people (including an estimated three million family units and many children and young people who are American citizens by birth). We should not simply round them up from the fields and the packing houses and send them packing.

Yet a further complicating twinge of conscience has afflicted other Democrats. They recognize that the burden of absorbing more and more immigrants into this country would fall unequally on Americans. The most vulnerable of citizens, already here legally, suffer the most from an oversupply of labor and the overtaxing of resources. Newly arriving immigrants have always threatened most grievously those who have the least secure hold on resources in the land.

Two moral problems cut across the ordinary lineups of the political parties on this particular issue. Whatever their party affiliation, the powerful are less willing to forgo the convenience of a steady supply of immigrants. They are tempted to downgrade the problem in the larger scheme of things, a response that subjects both immigrants and native workers to indifference and neglect. Meanwhile, those who are marginal are tempted, especially in hard times, to react with anger, resentment, and fear. The fears of the marginal tend to drive the debate today, but both the powerful and the marginal are complicit in our current plight.

The only solace in this political debate is that the battle lines do not tidily pit Democrats against Republicans. That arrangement would only further stiffen positions and block the way to compromise.

THE THEOLOGY OF THE STRANGER

I will not try to propose here a political program for dealing with undocumented workers. The contributions of theology to politics are more usually indirect rather than direct. However, the societies of both the ancient Middle East and North America have had to contend repeatedly with the vexing issue of the stranger. As an immigrant and perpetually migrant people, Americans have had to face the traumatic arrival of foreigners who, in wave after wave, have shocked the nervous system of those who preceded them. On this particular issue scripture and our deepest apprehensions connect.

Who is the stranger? The stranger is not the person who differs from me in incidental detail and costume. That is the doctrine behind the Enlightenment ideal of tolerance: the belief that beneath the stranger's odd clothing, someone just like me breathes. Therefore, live and let live, tolerate, learn to let go.

However, the stranger upsets the stable, familiar world that the preachers of tolerance presuppose. The experience is primordial. The earliest of mysterious warnings from parents invest the stranger with an unspecified power to do harm. Later in adult life the stranger is the person who unsettles my safeties, who hemorrhages my universe. He or she arouses uneasiness and aversion that can pass over into fright and enmity. Strangers are tricky. One would do well to give them a wide berth.

Before landing in this country the Puritans entered into their shipboard covenants to define their common life and safeties in a new land, but they discovered uneasily that the ground was already occupied by strangers (who surely viewed the Puritans as strangers). Soon thereafter, uninvited boatloads of immigrants arrived—Baptists and Jews and others. There goes the neighborhood. So the Puritans sent them off to Rhode Island. Governor John Winthrop wrote gloriously about the ligaments of love binding people together in their shipboard covenants, but he also wrote harshly on the subject of immigrants whom the Puritans banished from Massachusetts.[5]

Worse yet, those Puritans had children—the ultimate immigrants from the future, their squirming youngsters—who had not participated in those shipboard covenants but who now sat across the breakfast table from their aging parents. So the Puritans cobbled together their "half-way covenants" to accommodate their children and thus deal with their own generation gap opening out toward a future controlled by strangers.

When strangers are multiplied by the thousands or millions, they become those "foreigners" whose arrival in a country twitches the skin. They give the lie to the assumption that behind the stranger's impenetrable mask lies a familiar face, give or take a few wrinkles, as tolerable and acceptable as one's own. We do well to remember that in some languages the words for stranger and for enemy are one and the same.

Scripture calls for a response to the enemy that differs from the ideal of tolerance. Instead of relaxing one's attentiveness, as tolerance bids, the faith requires an intensifying of one's focus on the enemy. Do not solve your problem by driving your enemies to the edge of your mind. Let your enemies stand where they are. Now— love them; bless them that curse you; pray for them that spitefully use and persecute you. This is the strange task given to the church— without the promise, moreover, that love will somehow disarm your enemies and turn them into compliant friends. A system of justice distantly approximates this commandment of love when it insists that justice is blind; that is, justice does not open its eyes to lean preferentially toward those whom we recognize as our familiars.

In dealing further with the stranger in this closing chapter, I will not look with the eyes of those who feel threatened by the arrival of desperate immigrants, who worry that the stranger will edge them out, take their jobs, crowd their schools, or jump ahead of them in a very long queue. To take that view I would have to explore further the command to love one's enemies, those who seem vested with a power to destroy.

Instead, I will approach the issue from the perspective of the securely established and the powerful, for whom the immigrant offers not a threat but an opportunity—to get one's lawn cheaply mowed, meat butchered, children cared for, or bedridden elderly turned over and fed each day. That point of entry helps place covenantal love in the setting of justice. What do we owe the undocumented worker? What does the country owe at the same time to its own already documented working members? How do these obligations qualify one another?

Those questions emerge in a detail from the meatpacking plant raid in Iowa. The grandson of the plant owner appeared at a mass meeting following the government raid and explained that the company had already paid the workers what was owed to them. The plant had not reneged on their hourly wage. The court had not yet returned a verdict on the counter-allegations on this issue or on the charge that the company had violated child labor laws. The important point is that the grandson was appealing to the moral standard of a commercial contract.

Behind the company's appeal lay a basic vision of America as a nation defined largely by the arena of buying and selling. People are tied together by their contractual agreements with one another and by the government's agreement to enforce those contracts. That is what citizens have largely purchased through their taxes. Some have summed this up as the "contract with America."

Almost twelve million people have come here illegally. Many have had children here and have worked here, many of them fraudulently. By crossing the border and working here they broke our laws. We paid them anyway, but now it is time for them to go home. The obligations of buying and selling from our side have been kept. End of story.

Most of this book has argued that a different story honors better our ties to one another. We live in the arena of buying and selling, but the transactions of buying and selling depend upon the deeper exchanges of giving and receiving. Those exchanges supply the deeper tie that binds a people together. Our name for that tie has been not "contract" but "covenant."

No one recognized better than the novelist William Faulkner the difference between the external ties of contract and the deeper ties of covenant. His comic novel *Intruder in the Dust*, a story growing out of the scriptures of Israel, turned on an episode in which a white boy eventually becomes aware of the difference between the two human ties that have been the subject of this book.

At the outset of the novel the boy, hunting with young black friends, falls into a creek on a cold winter day. While thrashing about in the icy water he feels a long pole jab at his body and hears a commanding black voice say, "Boy, grab hold." A proud old black man, Lucas Beauchamp, brings the boy shivering back to his house, where Mrs. Beauchamp takes care of him. She takes off his wet clothes and wraps him in "Negro blankets" and feeds him "Negro food."

When his clothes dry out the boy dresses to go; but uneasy about the debt to the black man, he reaches into his pocket and pays Lucas off with seventy cents for his help. Lucas rejects the money firmly. The boy has obviously failed to get rid of his feeling of indebtedness. He tries furiously to recover his independence with token gifts, but the more exchanges occur between them, the deeper the uneasiness runs—until four years pass and town authorities falsely accuse Lucas of murdering a white man. They take Lucas to a jailhouse, where a crowd gathers and the boy, at the edge, watches the proceedings and ponders whether the old man remembers their earlier encounters. Just as Lucas is about to enter the jailhouse, he wheels and points toward the boy and says, "Boy, I want to see you." The boy obeys and visits Lucas, and eventually he and his aunt succeed in proving Lucas's innocence.

Faulkner's story serves as a parable for the relationship of blacks and whites in the South. Black men and women have labored in white men's fields. They have built and cared for their houses and fed, clothed, and nurtured their children. In accepting these labors the whites have received their life and substance from the blacks over and over again. But they resist this entanglement and want to pay off the blacks with a few marketplace coins. They try to define their relationship as contractual, transient, external, and shallow, to be managed at arm's length.[6]

For better or for worse, blacks and whites in this country have incorporated each other into their lives. Their destinies are intertwined. They cannot resolve the problem between them until they accept the deeper tie that the original receipt of labor entails. In the midst of buying and selling, a deeper giving and receiving occurs, altering the identity of each.

The scriptures of Israel are littered with such covenants and covenantal duties between humans, defined by that most singular covenant that embraces all others, the covenant of the people with God. The law instructs, in effect: When you harvest your crops, do not pick them too clean; leave some for the stranger for you were once strangers in Egypt. The structure of that imperative in Deuteronomy (24:19–22) makes it clear that giving is not a one-way street from giver to receiver—from the Jewish farmer to the stranger. That would be philanthropy. Rather, you should give as those who have richly received. You yourself were once strangers in Egypt, where you received the gift of deliverance. Now, you yourself give. The gift yields the task.

The story about the Jewish farmer takes place in the larger setting of the Old and New Covenants. For the Jews, the exodus was the gift, and the events of Mount Sinai, including all those repeated passages about sojourners and duties to sojourners, are part of the task. For Christians, death and resurrection is the gift, and the Sermon on the Mount, including all those repeated passages on loving the enemy and the needy, is the task. These duties to strangers are not just tacked onto a larger story.

Deuteronomy places strangers right there at Mount Sinai within sight and sound of the Israelites: "You stand . . . all of you before the Lord, your God—the heads of your tribes, your elders, and your officials . . . your little ones, your wives, and the sojourner who is in your camp, both he who hews your wood and he who draws your water . . . that he may establish you today as his people" (Dt 29:10–13).

In the New Testament, Jesus draws the stranger even closer to the heart of the covenantal command to love God with all our heart, soul, strength, and mind and to love our neighbor as ourself.

He supplies a parable in answer to the question, Who is my neighbor? The one who turns out to have neighbored me in the parable is a despised stranger, a Samaritan, who has shown kindness to me. He has expended himself for me. He is the neighbor I am called to love by doing likewise.

Living with this parable Christians recognize that Jesus is the strange neighbor whose self-expending love upsets their customary way of managing the world—like the priest and the Levite in the story, or like the lawyer who originally asks Jesus for the definition of a neighbor. Jesus is the ultimate stranger, the one who upsets my safeties, who threatens my daily pieties and rewrites my agenda. He is a threat to my ordinary religion ("he is a blasphemer") and to my ordinary morality ("he forgives sins"). His righteous death judges the unrighteousness of the people, and his death among the unrighteous judges the self-righteousness of the people. The crucifixion at the center of worship bars the Christian from relegating the command to love the stranger or the enemy to an afterthought in the Christian life. It is God's forethought, if you will. So one must understand it, if one begins where scripture begins: not simply with God's love of the stranger but with God's love *as* the stranger, a love by which the Christian recognizes him- or herself as judged and encouraged. John Calvin noted that the Good Samaritan story deprives the Christian of all grounds "for limiting the precept of love to one's own connections."[7]

The parable is embedded in American experience. As immigrants themselves Americans have received the huge gift of the labor and services of more than twelve million immigrants, who have labored on the cheap and some of whose kids have put down roots in the choir stalls of a St. Bridget's Church. The biblical narrative does not translate into legislation that dismisses any and all other considerations. However, it posts a powerful warning. Citizens cannot simply tell aliens whose labors they have greedily accepted that they must pull up their illegal roots and dry in the sun for ten years or so, while the nation builds a wall to seal out the unwanted. Americans cannot simply tear up what has transpired across decades with undocumented workers, pretend that nothing has happened, and punish them for fraud and identity theft and proceed to fracture deep human ties. We cannot simply deny the past and jail and deport millions of people. We have to work out our common life together. Our covenantal duties rest on a deeper footing than contract and on a lower pedestal than philanthropy.

Three guidelines have bearing upon the relations of people to strangers as they learn to work out their lives together: one, protect rather than exploit the vulnerable; two, respect others as self-determining rather than manipulate them as instruments; three, honor their excellences, even though their excellences may be alien to one's own. The first two guidelines are embedded in the received Western tradition. To protect rather than exploit the vulnerable draws on the recognizable principles of promoting the good and doing no harm. To respect others as self-determining (rather than manipulating them as instruments) draws on the familiar Kantian principle of respect for autonomy. However, the third guideline—to recognize and honor excellences, even those alien to one's own—most searchingly tests whether a host people will keep themselves open to what fully transpires in extended exchanges with strangers or strange cultures. The guideline recognizes that hosts are not merely actors but are acted upon in the course of their honoring others. One can sometimes protect and respect others without changing much oneself, but honoring the other in his or her alien excellence calls for an alteration in one's own sensibility as destinies intertwine.[8]

KEEPING COVENANT WITH DOCUMENTED WORKERS

We must face together an altered future with undocumented workers, whose labors we have ingested into our own lives. At the same time, we cannot simply forge policies that dismiss the fears of threatened Americans. We cannot continue a policy of lax borders to serve the convenience of prosperous people and pretend that we uphold thereby the liberality of an immigrant nation. The burden of that liberality falls too heavily on the most vulnerable and marginal, upon those with the least negotiating power and resource. We cannot simply require the working poor to pay the price for a better treatment of the desperate among the more recently arrived.

A prophetic message recorded in the Second Book of Samuel (11:1–12:9) supplies a further warning about how the powerful ought to behave in dealing with the powerless. Nathan, the prophet, upbraids King David, who has taken into his house the beautiful Bathsheba for his own while arranging to have her husband, Uriah the Hittite, killed in battle. Nathan traps David indirectly by asking for the king's judgment on the behavior of a rich man who feeds a hungry stranger not by giving him one of his own flock, but by taking the sole ewe lamb of his poor neighbor and handing it over to the hungry outsider. Just so, the powerful have concurrent obligations to the working poor, as they meet their obligations to the outsider. These obligations strain against one another and cannot be resolved simply to the advantage of the powerful. We cannot defect from one group on behalf of the other while leaving our own sheepfold untouched.

Senators Charles E. Schumer (D-NY) and Lindsey Graham (R-SC) collaborated on a 2010 article in the *Washington Post* to balance competing obligations.[9] They proposed four pillars for improvements in immigration law. The nation should act to improve border security (but not postpone all further reform until the borders were absolutely secure). It should create a fraud-resistant social security card for *all* workers eligible to work, and it should establish clear procedures for the admission of temporary workers. Finally, contrary to its characterization by the right, such a law would not declare a general amnesty for the millions of undocumented workers already here. However, it would establish a pathway to legal residency for those who wish to remain here, including such rigors as requiring them to admit that they have broken the law, to pay back taxes and fees, and to pass a criminal background check. As of this writing, polls suggest that the American people do not support passage of this bill, and Senator Graham, an original sponsor and key to bipartisan backing, withdrew his support on the grounds that such divisive legislation would not succeed in an election year.

Whatever the outcome of such legislation in any year, the existence of concurrent and conflicting obligations serves as a reminder that legislative action, no matter how Solomonic, is ragged. It leaves much unattended to in a very imperfect world. Undocumented workers expose the degree to which commitment to the civil covenant constantly needs repair.

THE CHURCH'S ROLE

Sister McCauley in Postville, Iowa, who said, "We need to see a collar here," recognized that the federal raid on the meatpacking plant shattered families and helped produce a catastrophe that transcended the limited world of politics. While the priest whom she had in mind was retired and out of town, her perception of need opens out on the vast territory of the spirit that lies beyond the reach of politics.

How small of all that human hearts endure,
That part which laws or kings can cause or cure.[10]

Samuel Johnson's couplet may be right in the cosmic scheme. It should remind the church that the health and vigor of the political arena requires further assists from the spirit on which inclusive community depends. However, Johnson's sigh should not lead religious people to diminish or despise the limited arena of politics or dismiss the distinctions between good and bad laws or the relative merit of competing remedies proposed.

For the most part, however, the capacity of religious communities to influence public policy *directly* is limited. Politicians have often discounted denominational lobbying, especially by the mainline Protestant churches. They know that the church's national leadership operates out of one ethos; lay people, by and large, operate out of another. Without effective teaching of their laity on issues of social justice, leaders in the mainline churches often seem to be all hat and no cattle.

Alternatively, some social activists in the churches on the left and the right have sought to influence the government indirectly through the media. To secure attention, they oblige the media's craving for visuals. They sometimes substitute placards and demonstrations for teaching their laity. This strategy tends to exclaim rather than explain, often angering rather than persuading readers and viewers. Such efforts constitute a kind of glossalalia on the right and the left, a speaking in tongues rather than in words that clarify and illumine the fateful choices of the day. A cry of pain gets attention, but it does not in and of itself reshape the community for remedy. It despairs of politics as the art of acting in concert with others for the common good.

Few theologians in the twentieth century emerged in religious communities and then acquired the status of public intellectuals with influence either in politics directly or in public culture more broadly. The exceptions were notable. Reinhold Niebuhr advanced a prophetic realism in American foreign and domestic policy. He influenced such public figures as George Kennan and Hubert Humphrey and cofounded Americans for Democratic Action. Niebuhr spelled out a cold-eyed realism about human nature and a progressive, rather than either a conservative or utopian, agenda in politics. Fr. John Courtney Murray, SJ, helped guide a long-delayed role for Roman Catholics in national politics. Fr. J. Bryan Hehir drafted the bishops' pastoral letter on nuclear war, which had an impact both within and far beyond the Catholic community.[11] Other Catholic intellectuals wrote accessibly to the wider public on such issues as economic justice and medical ethics. Martin Buber and Abraham Heschel also altered cultural professional sensibilities far beyond the measurable. Other less renowned Jewish leaders sustained a commitment to justice that traced back to the ancient prophets.

Most notably, Martin Luther King Jr. provided an exceptional public leadership for the black churches. He carried his constituency along with him as he rejected the black Muslim movement to his left and a centrist accommodation to his right and engaged in a disciplined civil disobedience. He relied brilliantly on the media to give him a wide public audience through civil rights protests, marches, and placards, but he also relied heavily on the spoken word to plead the justice of his cause, to discipline his followers, and to lead his opponents back to the conference table to effect change.

More traditionally, religious congregations have engaged in social action and service not through public debate, lobbying, organized protests, or the tracts of its intellectuals, but rather by appeal either to the doctrine of vocation or to the importance of corporal works of mercy. Structurally, the doctrine of vocation has been the more important Protestant appeal. Rightly understood and deployed, a vocation supplies the regular means of service to the neighbor and the common good. The professions, but not only the professions, constitute a lay ministry. Lay people should minister to others through their services as doctors, lawyers, carpenters, accountants, corporate and union leaders, politicians, journalists, and teachers. However, the slide of vocations into self-serving careers today has increased the difficulty of contributing to the common good through jobs alone.

The ancient tradition of corporal works of mercy has afforded the Catholic church, other churches, and voluntary communities with guideposts for service in response to chronic need (food, drink, clothing, shelter, care in times of sickness, and burial) as well as a charge to respond to occasional and extraordinary events (fire, flood, imprisonment, unemployment, and other misfortunes). The organized giving of time and money helps address the need for supplementary services beyond those supplied by professionals to hospitals, schools, and prisons. Such occasional and supplemental works of charity offer valued temporary relief.

Recently, some political conservatives have emphasized voluntary giving as a substitute for (and a reason for opposing) government action on major problems. However, social activists counter that enthusiasm for President George H. W. Bush's "thousand points of light" does not solve the deep structural problems a society faces. Personal charity falls short of love when one invokes the ideal of voluntary giving to oppose humane and just legislation.

This activist criticism of a volunteerism that opposes taxes is valid, but it overlooks the ways in which giving can also enlarge the giver. Voluntary giving can help motivate the pursuit of legislative remedies. Indeed, when lay people engage in hands-on service, the prospects for achieving further targeted legislation can improve. Direct lay experience can help create a more favorable ethos, atmosphere, and receptivity to such legislation. Although personal social service of the conventional sort may or may not tangibly benefit its recipients, it can help educate those performing the works of mercy. A ghetto suffers from economic poverty, but the white middle class suffers from impoverished experience. When horizons narrow to immediate experience, people shrink from the strange— the mentally defective, the prisoner, the aged, the ill, the culturally alien, the undocumented. Service, even of the amateur kind, can help create more experienced men and women whose lives are not as private, narrow, unimaginative, frightened, self-absorbed, and un-sympathetic. It can help create a leavening public within the public at large.

To this degree the church and other volunteer communities contribute to public culture—the ethos out of which better legislation can emerge. This contribution helps counter the tragic limitation of even well-intentioned politics. No given piece of legislation, like Schumer's immigrant reform bill, can be expected within the confines of the document alone to balance perfectly the interests of competing parties. Even at its best the reform will leave some needs unmet and some damages imposed. Other pieces of legislation may be required on still further issues—for example, crowded schools, neighborhoods, and health care clinics—to lessen the burden on vulnerable citizens already here. The task of the church is not simply to examine the legislation in isolation and pronounce it the best compromise possible but to remain open to yet further moves to make the original redress bearable.

Despite the best of intentions, political language, pointed toward particular interests, programs, and policies, inevitably sloganizes; it recoils, in the advertiser's horror, from the full complexity of experience. It boils down to talking points. It abstracts; and although its abstractions can clarify portions of the total consciousness of a people and help organize the government for action, slogans also distort, neglect, and marginalize other interests and ranges of conviction. Politics traffics only in the possible and the doable, not in the altogether. Its slogans inevitably denature reality; they grow distant and spectral; they captivate some followers but disconnect from others.

The tactical distortions and sloganizing of politics require the constant renewal of our common life: partly through art, partly through assorted voices at work in the several callings and voluntary communities, and partly through religion. A society needs its artists to help counter the manipulations of propaganda. In freshening language and perception artists help a society recover community in its entirety, which politicians risk sloganizing for the sake of immediate action.[12] Critical voices in the several callings of medicine, law, accounting, nursing, social work, teaching, engineering, business, and labor leadership and in the great spread of voluntary communities in this country can enliven and extend the work of a ministering justice. Religious congregations, engaged in self-expending service, can also help rescue the political community from a constant source of its perishing, keeping faith with their covenant by opening to the stranger and speaking on behalf of those who otherwise have no voice.

Of the voiceless there are always plenty—the repressed in hierarchical societies, the excluded in communitarian societies, and those hobbled at the gate in competitive, egalitarian societies. In its imperfection a nation that boldly declared at its outset, "We the People," recognizes some mix of all these faults in its own life, as it keeps covenant with the unfinished political agenda ahead.

NOTES

PREFACE

1. Spiegelberg, *Living Religions*, 451.
2. Hofstadter, *Paranoid Style*, 3–40.
3. See May, "Manichæism in American Politics."

CHAPTER 1

1. See Niccolò Machiavelli's prefatory letter to Lorenzo the Magnificent, son of Piero de Medici, in *Prince and the Discourses*, 4.
2. *Oxford Annotated Bible;* subsequent citations of the Bible refer to this edition.
3. Negatively interpreted, the Constitution was the creature of fear. Proponents feared that the failure to adopt the Constitution would mire the colonies in anarchy. Opponents feared that its adoption would create a powerful "central government similar to the one . . . [that the colonies] had only recently escaped from." Baylin, *To Begin the World Anew*, 107. More positively interpreted, the Constitution supplied a way of *containing* runaway fear. The structure of effective government with built-in restraints provided a way of containing runaway fear that would produce by way of overreaction to a specific evil—anarchy or tyranny—its opposite.
4. Centrists on the right and left also hold to their own differing definitions of the goods they rank first and second. For example, conservatives committed to law and order tend to confine economic justice to the enforcement of contracts, despite large inequalities in the relative power of the parties entering into contracts. Meanwhile, liberals committed to justice tend to define the social good of order by arrangements in the making, rather than by the root system of past ties.
5. See May, "Manichæism in American Politics."
6. See MacIntyre, *After Virtue*, 103.
7. See Gerth and Mills, *From Max Weber*, especially chap. 3, "Bureaucracy."
8. The ancient Manichæan myth inspired a theology of history that marked off cosmic conflict in three stages: (1) an original state of uneasy separation between the two rival powers, followed by (2) an aggravated period of their confusion and commingling, which could be

resolved only by (3) a final state of metaphysical apartheid in which the kingdom of righteousness will expel its rival, shear it of its aggressive power in open military contest, and in this sense achieve a final victory. Clearly the second stage, confusion, marks the worst state of affairs. Dualists want the lines clearly drawn. Negotiating compromises demeans and taints the purity of the righteous.

9. Kennan, *American Diplomacy*, 126. Still earlier, George Kennan had written that a self-confident America would give "the impression of coping successfully with the problems of its internal life." Ibid., 105. Kennan opposed negotiating with the Stalinists, but not for the categorical reason that dualists might have advanced. Rather Kennan believed that the Stalinists at the time would not (and could not) negotiate with the United States of America, because their purchase on power within the Soviet Union depended on defining the United States as their absolute enemy. The moment for negotiations had not yet arrived.

10. Kennan did not at that time recognize the long-range necessity for the virtue of temperance in restraining American appetites in economic policies, partly for the sake of American foreign policy. While Eurocentric (he supported the Marshall Plan for the reconstruction of Europe as serving our vital national interests), he did not yet recognize the long-range problems of global turmoil we stored up for ourselves as a nation controlling approximately 50 percent of the world's wealth with only 6.5 percent of the world's population.

11. See Gaddis, *Cold War.*

12. Thorkild Jacobsen, in Frankfort and others, *Before Philosophy*, 169.

13. See Walter, *Terror and Resistance.*

14. Frankfort and others, *Before Philosophy*, 194–95. Modern literature also varyingly associates water with the boundaryless, that is, the dangerously chaotic. Herman Melville in *Moby Dick* distinguishes Starbuck, the landlubber who cherishes and honors the settled boundaries and institutions of terra firma, from Ahab, the monomaniacal sea captain who forsakes all that is temperately human to pursue the whale. William Faulkner gives an account in *Wild Palms* of a rampaging Mississippi flood that exposes more than a seasonal eruption; it signals the primordial chaos that churns beneath all things.

15. While the boundless and potentially destructive character of water supplies a powerful and recurrent image for chaos, another two of the four basic elements supply us with yet further images: fire (which incinerates forms) and thin air (into which forms vanish). The destruction of the twin towers on 9/11 captured both. Further, the admixture

of water with the fourth element of earth (the mud of a quagmire or the festering of a swamp) provides two further images that figure in political rhetoric and strategies today.

16. The fear of death crowds people together and establishes the state, according to the Hobbesian account of origins. See Hobbes, *Leviathan*, chap. 13. While the later social contract theorist John Locke worked in less harsh language, he did not differ from Thomas Hobbes in his understanding of the origins of the state in a negative. People compact together and establish the state not because they want a common good, but because of the evils that would beset them had they remained in a state of nature. Life and property and freedom would be very "unsafe and insecure" and "full of fears and continual dangers" without the protection of the government. Locke, *Second Treatise of Government*, chap. 9, par. 123. Locke differed from Hobbes not in the account of the fear that inspires individuals to enter into the contract, but rather in the account of the rights that citizens retain to dissolve it. Citizens may dissolve or withdraw from the contract, if and as the sovereign should fail to keep his or her side of the bargain, either by failing to provide basic protection or by exercising additional, arbitrary powers.

17. John Hume, quoted in *Time*, January 29, 1973.

18. Arendt, *On Violence*, 79.

19. In the setting of nineteenth-century nihilism and anarchism, terrorism cannot be wholly understood as a political strategy. It also reflects a kind of religious ecstasy. Whatever the specifics of their religious traditions, terrorist leaders needing foot soldiers have sometimes depended upon ecstatics who stand outside the ordinary, practical world of means and ends. These foot soldiers enact a deed that has become an end in itself. Their action transcends the world of politics, and indeed this world altogether. Formally considered, the concept of an action that is an end in itself puts us rather close to the religious meaning of celebration. As Josef Pieper pointed out, "To celebrate a festival means to do something which is in no way tied up to other goals; it has been removed from all 'so that' and 'in order to.' True festivity cannot be imagined as residing anywhere but in the realm of activity that is meaningful *in itself.*" *In Tune with the World*, 7. In the case of terrorism, of course, the festival is a festival of death, a celebration that has its own priest and victim and that carries with it the likely risk that the attacker will become one of the victims. Today the rest of us become awed witnesses to this liturgical action through the medium of the media. Andre Malraux, drawing perhaps on the nihilists and anarchists but also on the romantics of the nineteenth century, captured better

than anyone else this religious/ecstatic encounter with death. In his novel *Man's Fate*, Malraux gave an account of a transfiguring encounter with death in the person of Che'en (9–19, 192–96, and 246–49). His fictional figure reflected and anticipated the earlier nineteenth-century and later twentieth-century nonfiction literature about terrorists. In the *Catechism of the Revolutionist*, variously attributed to the anarchists Sergei Nechaev and Mikhail Bakunin, the phrase "the revolutionist is a doomed man" is a repeated litany. "He must be ready to die at any moment." See Nomad, *Apostles of Revolution*, 228. The Algerian FLN (National Liberation Front), in its paper *Al Mondjahid* on August 20, 1957, observed, "As soon as the terrorist accepts the mission, death enters his soul. Henceforth he has a rendezvous with death." See Gaucher, *Terrorists*, 201.

20. Zinni, lecture.
21. For further details on systems disruption, see Robb, *Brave New War*, chap. 5. John Robb expressed little confidence in the nation-state as a provider of security and looked to local, decentralized, privatized, and crossconnected communities to provide security in the future. His visionary book reminds one of Simone Weil's proposals for the future of France, following World War II: decentralized and local. However, Robb's analysis lacked the more organic, communitarian spirit of Weil's vision in *Need for Roots*.
22. Shapiro, *Containment*, 37.
23. Ibid., 76–89.
24. Nye, *Paradox of American Power*, 4–12.
25. Fanon, *Wretched of the Earth*, 43.
26. See Phillips, *American Theocracy*, chaps. 1–3.
27. Amy Chua, for example, saw tolerance as an important key to legitimacy (and longevity) in her comparative study of empires, *Day of Empire*.
28. Keegan and Kristol, *Present Dangers*, 5, 15, 16.
29. Johnson, *Sorrows of Empire*, 4.
30. Brzezinski, *Choice*, 213.
31. Goldsmith, *Terror Presidency*, 165.
32. Ibid., 71. As head of the Central Intelligence Agency, George Tenet also wrote, "[You] simply could not sit where I did and read what passed across my desk . . . and be anything but scared to death about what it portended." Quoted in ibid., 72. In a similar vein former Deputy Attorney General Jim Comey averred, "Reading about plans for chemical and biological and nuclear attacks . . . causes you to imagine a threat so severe that it becomes an obsession." Quoted in ibid.
33. Dick Cheney, quoted in Suskind, *One Percent Doctrine*, 62. Cheney offered this view in a late November 2001 meeting with Secretary of

State Condoleezza Rice, Tenet, and a Tenet briefer in attendance. One or both of the latter two must have been Ron Suskind's source.

34. Arthur Schlesinger Jr., quoted in Dallek, *Nixon and Kissinger,* 613–23.
35. Henry Kissinger, quoted in ibid., 297.
36. Brzezinski, *Second Chance,* 155. The neoconservatives have countered this classical conservative warning about the difficulty of imposing democracy on other countries by pointing to the successful transplant in West Germany and Japan after World War II. Allied successes there prove that outside interventions supporting democracy do not inevitably fail. However, critics have made distinctions between the cases. Iraq lacked the basic coherence and common memories on which the other two countries could build.
37. The difficulties of recasting the world in our own image came home dramatically in 2007 in the premiere episode of the public television series *America at a Crossroad.* Host Robert MacNeil showed a clip of an American motivational trainer trying to drum into Iraq's troops the president's message of freedom. The trainer got them shouting over and over again, in unison, "Freedom, freedom, freedom." He resembled a high school football coach juicing up his players before sending them out into the red zone of the gridiron—to little avail. Culturally the opposite of tyranny for the Iraqis (as for the Israelites of the First Book of Samuel) is not freedom but justice. The religious right in the Middle East has preached obedience, not freedom, and theocracy, not democracy. Liberty, they fear, leads to chaos, not justice. Simply gagging them with our word "freedom" is not likely to leave a democracy blooming in the desert or on the streets of Baghdad.
38. Caspar Weinberger, quoted in Savage, *Takeover,* 60. The foregoing paragraph draws on Charlie Savage's book for some of the events diminishing presidential power that prompted Cheney's subsequent actions as vice president.
39. Ibid., 102.
40. Hamilton, Madison, and Jay, *Federalist Papers,* nos. 69 and 70. Subsequent citations of the *Federalist Papers* appear in the text.
41. See Yoo, *Crisis and Command* and *Powers of War and Peace.*
42. Wills, "At Ease, Mr. President."
43. Auden, *New Year Letter,* 40.
44. Quentin Anderson, *Imperial Self.*
45. Adler and Gorman, *American Testament,* 87.
46. See Wood, *Creation of the American Republic,* 68.
47. Augustine, *Against the Epistle of Manichæus,* chaps. 1–3.
48. Ibid., 29.

CHAPTER 2

1. Congressional Budget Office data analyzed and quoted in Phillips, *Wealth and Democracy*, 128–29. This transfer of effective wealth increased unabated in the 2000s, when President George W. Bush cut the income tax rate and phased down the estate tax in 2001 and reduced taxes on dividends and capital gains in 2003. See Congressional Budget Office, "Historical Federal Effective Tax Rates."

2. Since the 1960s we have defined as "poor" those whose income falls short of three times their estimated food costs. In fact, food costs have always been lower than one-third of a total budgetary need. Meanwhile, housing, transportation, and child care costs for the working poor have skyrocketed. The actual poor outnumber the officially poor, and children constitute a much higher percentage of the poor than the elderly do. See Ehrenreich, *Nickel and Dimed*, 200.

3. Toynbee, *Study of History*, 375–403.

4. Ehrenreich, *Nickel and Dimed*, 221.

5. Reich, *Work of Nations*, 291.

6. See Cassidy, "Greed Cycle," 77. Chief executives also secured advance access to initial public offerings from investment houses eager to lure business in their direction.

7. In his lengthy article "Triple-A Failure," reporter Roger Lowenstein analyzed one such mortgage "security" that included 2,393 subprime mortgages with a total face value of $430 million. Three-quarters of the borrowers had adjustable rate mortgages; almost half provided no written verification of incomes; and nearly half simultaneously took out a second mortgage on the home, instantly yielding no owner's equity in the property. A reporter for the *Wall Street Journal* for more than a decade, Lowenstein later published a book-length narrative on the financial train wreck ahead titled *The End of Wall Street*.

8. Michael Lewis reported, "The rating agencies had abandoned their posts . . . they were almost surely rating their CDOs without knowing what was inside them." *Big Short*, 177. Lewis's book, along with Lowenstein's *End of Wall Street*, was helpful in summarizing the run-up and collapse of the real estate market boom in this chapter.

9. Phillips, *Wealth and Democracy*, 412. Lewis also captured in *Big Short* the psychic distance between action and material consequence: "That was the problem with money: What people did with it had consequences, but they were so remote from the original action that the mind never connected the one with the other." 251.

10. "Since 1913, the United States has witnessed only one other year of such unequal wealth distribution—1928, the year before the stock market crashed." Jenny Anderson, "Hedge Fund Managers."

11. Friedman, "Green the Bailout."
12. Lindblom, "Privileged Position," especially 171–75. Business, however, hugely differs from the medieval church and from most governments. Only particular corporations, not the larger marketplace itself, are organized, internally subordinated institutions. Business looks chiefly to the mechanism of the marketplace, rather than to a particular business institution, as the basic allocator of power. Within the setting of this mechanism institutions and their leaders may rise and fall, but the mechanism itself draws the basic fealty of the multiple players.
13. See Parker, "Government beyond Barack Obama."
14. For details on the gaming of the tax and regulatory systems, see Lewis and Allison, *Cheating of America*, 260ff. For the Enron gaming of the Securities and Exchange Commission, the State of California, their employees, and many others, see McLean and Elkind, *Smartest Guys*.
15. Lewis, *Big Short*, 223.
16. For this analysis of the two types of love of money, see Skidelsky, *Keynes*, 142. Robert Skidelsky, as the author of an earlier three-volume biography of Lord John Maynard Keynes, had access to his subject's unpublished papers, quoted here.
17. Ibid.
18. See Keynes, *General Theory of Employment*, 372–73.
19. The hospice image comes from John Diercie, executive director for policy at the Financial Services Forum, cited by Sewell Chan in his excellent summary article "Finding the Way to the Final Bill."
20. Lewis and Allison, *Cheating of America*, 261.
21. Calmes and Story, "Outcry Builds in Washington."
22. Chernow, "Of Avarice and Enterprise," 344–47, 358–59.
23. William Lee Miller, author of *Lincoln's Virtues* and *President Lincoln*, drew my attention to Abraham Lincoln's fragment on government (also found in *The Collected Works of Abraham Lincoln*, vol. 2, edited by Roy P. Basler, 220–21).
24. Obama, "What the People Need Done."
25. *Lincoln Savings and Loan Association v. Wall.* The actual paraphrase above the main entrance to the Internal Revenue Service's headquarters in the District of Columbia reads "Taxes are what we pay for a civilized society."

CHAPTER 3

1. For an expanded account of the public responsibilities of the professions, the universities, religious congregations, and the media, see May, *Beleaguered Rulers*.
2. Pound, *Lawyer*, 5.

3. Susan P. Koniak, professor of law at the Boston University School of Law, gave testimony titled "Where Were the Lawyers? Behind the Curtain Wearing Their Magic Caps" on February 6, 2002. See US Senate, *Hearing on Accountability Issues.*

4. The economist Paul Krugman devoted three key chapters in his book *Conscience of a Liberal* to politics—and not a single chapter to economics—to emphasize that political, not economic, factors moved American society toward and then away from equality in the Roosevelt and Reagan eras. Thus the economist dismissed economic determinism. See his chapters titled "The Politics of the Welfare State," "The Politics of Inequality," and "The New Politics of Equality."

5. The advantages of Catholic polity and finances in facing the issue of race relations may have proved a disadvantage later in the century when it came to dealing with priestly sexual abuse. The existence of discretionary funds at the diocesan level under the control of the bishop may have allowed some bishops to let their concern for "avoiding scandal" outweigh the necessity of prompt action on sexual abuse, until at length the problem of sexual abuse (and the scandal, now much magnified) exploded churchwide. Heavier lay involvement in church finances at the local level might have led to a more prompt response to the problem. No polity spares its members the task of dealing with temptation.

6. Phillips, *American Theocracy*, xiv. See also ibid., chap. 6, "The United States in a Dixie Cup: the New Religious and Political Battlegrounds."

7. Wallis, *God's Politics.*

8. National Conference of Catholic Bishops, *Challenge of Peace*; John Paul II, *Laborem exercens*; National Conference of Catholic Bishops, *Economic Justice for All.*

9. Cafardi, Kaveny, and Kmiec, "A Catholic Brief for Obama."

10. See Kaveny, "Intrinsic Evil and Political Responsibility."

11. Pew Forum on Religion and Public Life, "Voting Religiously."

12. Bell, *Cultural Contradictions of Capitalism*, xxv.

13. Kierkegaard, "Present Age," 267; see Postman, *Amusing Ourselves to Death.*

CHAPTER 4

1. Augustine, *Confessions*, 47, 237ff. Subsequent citations in the text refer to the book and paragraph numbers rather than to page numbers, in the Sheed translation.

2. Huizinga, *Waning of the Middle Ages.*

3. Auden, *New Year Letter*, 40.

4. Bush, quoted in Bacevich, *Limits of Power*, 60.

5. Donald Rumsfeld, quoted in Bacevich, *Limits of Power*, 58–59.

6. In 1975 Anthony Sampson linked directly "the West's dependence upon energy . . . with the whole character of the future Western life-style." *Seven Sisters*, 373.
7. Bush, State of the Union address. Thirty-three years before George W. Bush's address, Sampson predicted, "There is a real danger that the Western countries will become crippled by their indebtedness to this one seductive and fickle source of energy." *Seven Sisters*, 373. Or again the Western public must avoid the "technological trap" of "becoming caught up in an extravagant life style which they will not be able to afford, either economically or politically." *Seven Sisters*, 380.
8. Tamminen, *Lives per Gallon*, 62–63.
9. Ibid., 109.
10. See ibid., 129. In response to the assertion by Paul Baily, the American Petroleum Institute's director of health and environmental affairs, that "people exposed to ozone actually adapt to it," Tamminen wryly noted, "Ozone acts like an acid on the lungs. . . . Twenty thousand premature deaths are a rather extreme form of 'adaptation.'"
11. Ibid., 110.
12. Pollan, *Omnivore's Dilemma*, 45. Michael Pollan's book artfully traces meals that might actually appear on a dinner table back to the larger shifts from organic to petrochemical agriculture. He describes Sir Albert Howard's influence on the green movement protest against industrial agriculture in ibid., 145–46. See also the innumerable collections of essays by Wendell Berry, the leading agrarian, to get a sense of the green movement protest in full and eloquent voice: for example, *Art of the Commonplace* and *Citizenship Papers*.
13. Wilson, "Last Bite," 97.
14. See Gawande, "Testing, Testing," 34–41.
15. For the analysis of the sins of pride and acquisitiveness in the context of anxiety, see Niebuhr, *Nature and Destiny of Man*, 1:7.
16. Daniel Gross gives this brief description of Robert H. Frank's theory of "positional" goods in his essay "No Rest for the Wealthy." Frank and Philip J. Cook developed the theory of positional goods in *Winner-Take-All Society*, 41–42, 57–58, 82–84, 173–74, 178–180.
17. See Shiller, "Animal Spirits Depend on Trust."
18. See Niebuhr, *Nature and Destiny of Man*, 1:7, and Tillich, *Courage to Be*, 64–70, for their roughly comparable treatments of failing strategies in the face of anxiety.

CHAPTER 5

1. Matthewes, lecture.
2. Hobbes, *Leviathan*, 13:143.

3. Locke, *Second Treatise of Government*, 9:123.
4. Ibid., 9:127.
5. Macpherson, *Political Theory*, 263.
6. Winthrop, "A Model of Christian Charity," 89.
7. See Beard, *Economic Interpretation of the Constitution*, and conservative criticism of Beard's view by McDonald, *We the People*.
8. Countryman, *What Did the Constitution Mean*, 20.
9. Morgan, *American Heroes*, 223.
10. James Madison to William Eustis, July 6, 1819, quoted in Rakove, "The Perils of Originalism."
11. Flannery O'Connor wrote, "A people is known, not by its statements or its statistics, but by the stories it tells." *Mystery and Manners*, 192.
12. Arendt, *On Revolution*, 124–37.
13. In her book on the three revolutions—American, French, and Russian—Arendt argued that the American Revolution alone succeeded in overcoming tyranny. The French rebelled against an oppressive regime but ended up with Napoleon. The Russians took dead aim on the tzar and the Russian nobility only to spend the next seventy years in the grip of Stalin and his successors. The failure of these revolutions carries a message. A negative protest against misery and oppression will not in itself carry a society forward into reconstructing its life. The Americans, however, succeeded. The revolutionaries did not simply reinstall a domestic version of King George III when they overthrew British rule. Drawing on their own prior experience in self-government, they launched a republic. See ibid., chaps. 2–4.
14. See Elazar, *Covenant Tradition in Politics*, vol. 1, chap. 10.
15. Elazar wrote, "In the Christian tradition, as it was taken over by the Catholic and Orthodox Churches, the political dimension of the new covenant came to be understood in oligarchic and hierarchical terms. In that respect, emphasis on covenant as a matter of God's graciousness rather than mutual agreement lent itself to a more hierarchical approach to human government, especially since government was considered an institution that existed only because of man's sinfulness and, therefore, as a punishment of God and not an instrument of human fulfillment." *Covenant Tradition in Politics*, vol. 2, 48.
16. On the merits Israel was not much to look at. Hosea and Ezekiel make that clear. On the day of her birth Israel was weltering in her blood, but God chose Israel and lavished on her care and attention and eventually a discipline, as the people covenanted with God at Mount Sinai. There the people accepted a set of duties, of faithfulness in performance and generosity toward their fellows and toward strangers that

might not have occurred to people who smugly viewed their identity as their achievement, a reward for hard work.

17. Elazar, *Covenant Tradition in Politics*, vol. 1, 193.
18. A group of scholars, including Rozann Rothman, has emerged today to claim that though the "rhetoric of the Constitution was the rhetoric of contract and compact . . . the Constitution was permeated with the substance of covenant which anchored and perpetuated the commitment to the Union" (Rothman, "Impact of Covenant," 63).
19. Ibid., 29.
20. Calvin, *Institutes of the Christian Religion*, 4:20:3, 652.
21. Sheldon Wolin titles the sixth chapter of his book *Politics and Vision* "Calvin: The Political Education of Protestantism."
22. Calvin, *Institutes of the Christian Religion*, 4:20:18, 666.
23. Ibid., 3:7:1, 7.
24. Ibid., 3:7:5, 10. Calvin continued to link gifts, gratitude, stewardship, and love: "In regard to everything which God has bestowed upon us and by which we aid our neighbor, we are stewards and are bound to give an account of our stewardship; moreover, that the only right mode of administration is that which is regulated by love."
25. Ibid. Calvin mocked "the absurd description which the Stoics of old gave of their hero as one who, divested of humanity, was affected in the same way by adversity and prosperity, grief and joy; or rather, like a stone, was not affected by anything." 3:8:9, 21.
26. Calvin preferred the Apostle Paul to the Stoics in recognizing natural feeling: "We are troubled on every side, yet not distressed; we are perplexed, but not in despair; persecuted, but not forsaken; cast down, but not destroyed." 2 Corinthians 4:8, 9; cited in ibid.
27. Calvin, *Institutes of the Christian Religion*, 3:7:8, 13.

CHAPTER 6

1. See Breyer, *Active Liberty*, 3–34 and 133–35. Justice Stephen Breyer wrote that "active liberty, the principle of participatory self government" rather than the libertarian principle of negative liberty, a freedom from restraint, "was the primary force shaping the system of government that the document creates." 21. In pressing the overriding theme of active liberty Breyer rejected the method of the "Originalists" on the Court who, to defend their views, engage in a kind of fundamentalist removal of a particular text from its context in the document as a whole. He likened the task of a Supreme Court justice to that of the conductor of a symphony orchestra, who is obliged to interpret the musical notes within the setting of the whole score—to

interpret the text within the setting of context; or as preachers would recognize, to discern the Word in the words.

2. Libertarian advocates of negative liberty reject interference from outside human agency. Liberty should be limited, but only to the degree that it interferes with the negative liberty of others. The Bill of Rights purportedly protects individuals from the alien intrusions of government. It tends to link freedom with indeterminacy. In moderate liberal theory negative liberty enjoys priority as the precondition and presupposition of positive liberty. Only if freedom is a freedom *from* is it possible and meaningful for it to be a freedom *to* or *for.*

Positive freedom has a normative content. It offers imperatives that should shape the actual uses of freedom. The specifics of that content depend upon whether the emphasis falls on freedom *to* or *for.* Freedom *to* places the emphasis on the goal of self-mastery. It recognizes that the self may be free from the interference of an external agency but not yet fully itself. It has not yet reached its maturity. It has not yet won all battles with itself in the pursuit of its own best interests and goods. Liberal theorists have worried about the dangers of letting some positive societal notion of the fulfilled self, the higher self, compromise the principle of negative liberty. Along that route, they fear, the norms of a given class, party, race, religion, leader, or generation tend to dominate others. Negative liberty is lost, and with it the self's positive freedom and responsibility to determine its own wants and goods. External restraints on the self for the self's own good describe a paternalism that the libertarian eschews. For an eloquent statement of the libertarian perspective see Berlin, "Two Concepts of Liberty."

Yet another view emerges if positive freedom means a freedom *for* in the sense of a freedom to be for others. This vision is more communitarian than those that emphasize either a freedom from or a freedom to. This perspective would not site manhood and womanhood in a zone of indeterminacy in which the self can move largely as it pleases, nor would this perspective lie in some vision of self-mastery in which the self lifts off only in those directions that lead to ever richer drafts of freedom. Rather the self flourishes more fully as itself in its capacity to be with and for others.

Reflexively this communitarian vision also calls for a high regard for negative freedom. One must be free from many kinds of constraints to be fully free for others. Community itself does not fully flourish without negative liberty. The trouble with slavery is not simply that the master fails to be for the slave; the slave also fails to be for the master. The more the master compels the slave, the more the slave pulls more deeply into himself. Georg Wilhelm Friedrich Hegel and Karl Marx, long ago, and subsequent writers on enslavement (Martin Luther King Jr. included) knew that slavery fails not only by virtue of its insufficiency of freedom (in the sense of negative liberty) but by its lack of community (in the sense of the freedom to be for one another).

3. Elazar, *Covenant Tradition in Politics*, vol. 1, 339.

4. The historian William Lee Miller used the contrasting phrases from the philosopher David Hume ("calmly realistic" rather than "fiercely pessimistic") to characterize the realism about human nature to which Madison subscribed. See Miller, *Business of May Next*, 56. In my paragraphs on Madison I have relied on Miller's impressive argument (chaps. 2–4 and especially chap. 15) showing that Madison took realism in a progressive rather than a conservative direction.

5. Ibid., 32.

6. Ibid., 222–23.

7. Ibid., 230.

8. Madison, quoted in Wood, *Creation of the American Republic*, 65–69.

9. "No phrase except 'liberty' was invoked more often than 'public good.'" Adler and Gorman, *American Testament*, 87.

10. Montesquieu, *Spirit of the Laws*, 1:3, 19–28.

11. Edwards, "A Treatise," 520.

12. Edwards, "Some Thoughts," 265. Jonathan Edwards wanted to move beyond the "flash and noise" of the revivals to the place where holy affection becomes habitual and spurs the self not toward self-absorption or idolatry but toward a benevolence to being in general, which in true virtue is immediately exercised in a general good will.

13. Cooper, "Sermon Preached before His Excellency John Hancock."

14. Benjamin Rush, quoted in Heimert, *Religion and the American Mind*, 529.

15. Nathaniel Niles, quoted in ibid., 515.

16. Ibid., 511.

17. Edwards, "Some Thoughts," 272–73.

18. Alexis de Tocqueville's statement on the covenantal spirit in America restricted moral obligation rather too narrowly to personal assistance to others. It left untouched the injustices in structures that persisted in the 1840s, most particularly the harshest of those structures, the institution of slavery. It also left potentially untouched the structural injustices of an expanding industrial economy that would follow the Civil War. See Tocqueville, *Democracy in America*.

19. Morgan, *American Heroes*, 223.

20. Miller, *Business of May Next*, 64.

CHAPTER 7

1. The forty-ninth Arizona Legislature passed Senate Bill 1070 concerning the enforcement of immigration laws in its second regular session of 2010. See Archibold, "Arizona Enacts Stringent Law."

2. According to Julia Preston, in her article "Decline Seen in Numbers of People Here Illegally," the estimated number of "illegals" may have declined in the United States in a single year, from a peak of 12.5 million in 2007 to 11.2 million in 2008. The Center for Immigration Studies, she noted, may have exaggerated both the top figure in 2007 and the decline of 1.3 million by July 2008. The Center, as an advocacy group, wanted to emphasize the magnitude of the problem and the importance of border control as a solution. Other commentators have argued that the decline of the American economy may have contributed more than policing did to the decrease of illegals in the United States.

3. Preston, "Interpreter Speaking Up." For what follows in this chapter on the facts of the Postville raids, I have relied on Preston's reports in the *New York Times*.

4. Samuel G. Freedman, in his article "Immigrants Find Solace after Storm of Arrests," called Sister Mary McCauley a pastor administrator, though I understand the generally more correct term is "parish administrator." He supplied the other details in this paragraph, including her vivid summons: "We need to see a collar here."

5. Compare John Winthrop's sermon "A Model of Christian Charity" (1630) with his "A Declaration in Defense of an Order of Court Made in May 1637," referring to a court order restricting immigration in the case of such troubling persons as Anne Hutchinson.

6. For further exploration of Faulkner's *Intruder in the Dust* in the setting of professional ethics, see May, *The Physician's Covenant*, 128–29.

7. Calvin, *Institutes of the Christian Religion*, vol. 1, 2:7:55, 359.

8. Charles Taylor has explored in several books this third element of the interaction of cultures strange to one another. See his *Sources of the Self*, most accessibly, chap. 5, "The Need for Recognition," in his *Ethics of Authenticity*; and most extensively, his long essay titled "The Politics of Recognition," to which Jürgen Habermas, Michael Walzer, and others have responded in Gutmann, *Multiculturalism*. Taylor has grounded his argument for what I have called "honoring alien excellences" in the Canadian effort to absorb diverse cultures—Anglo, French, and Inuit—into its life.

9. Schumer and Graham, "Right Way to Mend Immigration."

10. Samuel Johnson wrote these lines of poetry for Oliver Goldsmith's "The Traveller," quoted in Bates, *Samuel Johnson*, 218.

11. Fr. J. Bryan Hehir drafted the US Catholic bishops' pastoral letter titled *The Challenge of Peace: God's Promise and Our Response* for a committee of bishops chaired by Cardinal Joseph Bernardin of Chicago with significant input from Bishop Thomas Gumbleton of Detroit. The final text was approved by the then National Conference of Catholic Bishops meeting in plenary assembly in Chicago on May 3, 1983. See also Richard B. Miller, "Final Draft of the Pastoral Letter," for a nuanced account of refinements in Catholic reflection on nuclear war.
12. See Collingwood, *Principles of Art*.

BIBLIOGRAPHY

Adler, Mortimer J., and William Gorman. *The American Testament.* New York: Praeger Publishers, 1975.

Anderson, Jenny. "Hedge Fund Managers Get Billion-Dollar Paydays." *New York Times,* April 16, 2005.

Anderson, Quentin. *The Imperial Self: An Essay in American Literary and Cultural History.* New York: Alfred A. Knopf, 1971.

Archibold, Randal C. "Arizona Enacts Stringent Law on Immigration." *New York Times,* April 24, 2010.

Arendt, Hannah. *On Revolution.* New York: Viking Press, 1963.

———. *On Violence.* New York: Harcourt, Brace and World, 1969.

Auden, W. H. *New Year Letter.* London: Faber and Faber, 1941.

Augustine. *Against the Epistle of Manichæus Called Fundamental.* Translated by Richard Stothert. In *The Nicene and Post-Nicene Fathers: First Series,* edited by Philip Schaff. Vol. 4. Grand Rapids, MI: William B. Eerdmans Publishing Company, 1956.

———. *Confessions of St. Augustine.* Translated by F. J. Sheed. New York: Sheed and Ward, 1943.

Bacevich, Andrew J. *The Limits of Power.* New York: Metropolitan Books, Henry Holt and Company, 2008.

Bartlett, Bruce. *Imposter.* New York: Doubleday, 2006.

Bates, W. Jackson. *Samuel Johnson.* New York: Harcourt Brace Jovanovich, 1975.

Baylin, Bernard. *To Begin the World Anew: The Genius and Ambiguity of the Founders.* New York: Vintage Books, 2004.

Beard, Charles A. *An Economic Interpretation of the Constitution of the United States.* New York: Macmillan, 1913.

Before Philosophy. Middlesex, England: Penguin Books, 1951.

Bell, Daniel. *The Cultural Contradictions of Capitalism.* New York: Basic Books, Inc., 1976.

Berlin, Isaiah. "Two Concepts of Liberty." In *Four Essays on Liberty.* London: Oxford University Press, 1969. Originally given as inaugural lecture, Oxford University, October 31, 1958.

Berry, Wendell. *The Art of the Commonplace.* Emeryville, CA: Shoemaker and Hoard, 2002.

————. *The Citizenship Papers: Essays by Wendell Berry.* Washington, DC: Shoemaker and Hoard, 2003.

Breyer, Steven. *Active Liberty: Interpreting our Democratic Constitution.* New York: Vintage Books, 2006.

Brzezinski, Zbigniew. *The Choice: Global Dominion or Global Leadership.* New York: Basic Books, 2004.

————. *Second Chance: Three Presidents and the Crisis of American Super-power.* New York: Basic Books, 2007.

Bush, George W. State of the Union address, Washington, DC, January 31, 2006. www.cbsnews.com/stories/2006/01/31/politics/main1264706. shtml

Cafardi, Nicholas, Cathleen Kaveny, and Douglas W. Kmiec. "A Catholic Brief for Obama." *Newsweek,* October 17, 2008. www.newsweek.com/2008/10/16/a-catholic-brief-for-obama.html.

Calmes, Jackie, and Louise Story. "Outcry Builds in Washington for Recovery of AIG Bonuses." *New York Times,* March 18, 2009.

Calvin, John. *The Institutes of the Christian Religion.* London: James Clarke & Co. Limited, 1953.

Camus, Albert. *The Rebel.* New York: Vintage Books, 1956.

Cassidy, John. "The Greed Cycle." *The New Yorker,* September 23, 2002.

Chan, Sewell. "Finding the Way to the Final Bill." *New York Times,* May 22, 2010.

Chernow, Ron. "Of Avarice and Enterprise." Chap. 18 in *Alexander Hamilton.* New York: Penguin Press, 2004.

Chua, Amy. *Day of Empire: How Hyperpowers Rise to Global Dominance and Why They Fall.* New York: Doubleday, 2007.

Clarke, Richard A. *Against All Enemies: Inside America's War on Terror.* New York: Free Press, 2004.

Collingwood, R. G. *The Principles of Art.* Oxford: Clarendon Press, 1938.

Congressional Budget Office. "Historical Federal Effective Tax Rates: 1979 to 2004." www.cbo.gov/doc.cfm?index=7718.

Cooper, Samuel. "A Sermon Preached before His Excellency John Hancock." Boston, 1780. Quoted in Hatch, *The Sacred Cause of Liberty,* 105.

Countryman, Edward. *What Did the Constitution Mean to Early Americans?* Boston and New York: Bedford/St. Martins, 1999.

Dallek, Robert. *Nixon and Kissinger: Partners in Power.* New York: Harper-Collins, 2007.

Edwards, Jonathan. "Some Thoughts concerning the Present Revival of Religion in New England." In Heimert and Miller, *The Great Awakening.*

————. "A Treatise Concerning Religious Affections." In Heimert and Miller, *The Great Awakening.*

Ehrenreich, Barbara. *Nickel and Dimed: On (Not) Getting By in America.* New York: Henry Holt and Company, 2001.

Elazar, Daniel J. *The Covenant Tradition in Politics.* Vol. 1, *Covenant and Polity in Biblical Israel.* New Brunswick, NJ: Transaction Publishers, 1995.

———. *The Covenant Tradition in Politics.* Vol. 2, *Covenant and Commonwealth.* New Brunswick, NJ: Transaction Publishers, 1995.

Fama, Eugene. "Efficient Capital Markets." *Journal of Finance* (May 1970). Quoted in Fox, *Myth of the Rational Market,* 104.

Fanon, Franz. *The Wretched of the Earth.* New York: Grove Press, 1968.

Faulkner, William. *Intruder in the Dust.* New York: Random House, 1948.

———. *Wild Palms.* New York: Random House, 1939.

Ferguson, Niall. *Colossus: The Price of America's Empire.* New York: Penguin Press, 2004.

Fox, Justin. *The Myth of the Rational Market: A History of Risk, Reward, and Delusion on Wall Street.* New York: HarperCollins, 2009.

Frank, Robert H., and Philip J. Cook. *The Winner-Take-All Society.* New York: Free Press, 1995.

Frankfort, Henri, H. A. Frankfort, John A. Wilson, and Thorkild Jacobsen. *Before Philosophy: The Intellectual Adventure of Ancient Man.* Middlesex, England: Penguin Books, 1951.

Freedman, Samuel G. "Immigrants Find Solace after Storm of Arrests." *New York Times,* July 12, 2008.

Friedman, Thomas L. "Green the Bailout." *New York Times,* September, 28, 2008.

Gaddis, John Lewis. *The Cold War: A New History.* New York: Penguin Press, 2005.

———. *Strategies of Containment.* New York: Oxford University Press, 2005.

Gaucher, Roland. *The Terrorists.* Translated by Paula Spurlin. London: Secker and Warburg, 1968.

Gawande, Atul. "Testing, Testing: The Health-Care Plan Has No Master Plan for Curbing Costs. Is That a Bad Thing?" *The New Yorker,* December 14, 2009.

Gerth, H. H., and C. Wright Mills, trans. and ed. *From Max Weber: Essays in Sociology.* New York: Oxford University Press, 1958.

Gilder, George. *Wealth and Poverty.* New York: Basic Books, 1981.

Goldsmith, Jack. *The Terror Presidency: Law and Judgment inside the Bush Administration.* New York: W. W. Norton & Company, 2007.

Gordon, David M. *Fat and Mean.* New York: Free Press, 1996.

Gordon, Michael R., and Bernard E. Trainor. *Cobra II: The Inside Story of the Invasion of Iraq.* New York: Pantheon Books, 2006.

Gross, Daniel. "No Rest for the Wealthy." *New York Times Book Review,* July 1, 2009.

Gutmann, Amy, ed. *Multiculturalism: Examining the Politics of Recognition.* Princeton, NJ: Princeton University Press, 1994.

Hamilton, Alexander, James Madison, and John Jay. *The Federalist Papers.* New York: New American Library, 1961.

Hatch, Nathan O. *The Sacred Cause of Liberty: Republican Thought and the Millennium in Revolutionary New England.* New Haven, CT: Yale University Press, 1977.

Heimert, Alan. *Religion and the American Mind: From the Great Awakening to the Revolution.* Cambridge, MA: Harvard University Press, 1966.

Heimert, Alan, and Perry Miller, ed. *The Great Awakening: Documents Illustrating the Crisis and Consequences.* Indianapolis, IN: Bobbs-Merrill Company, Inc, 1967.

Hobbes, Thomas. *Leviathan.* Cleveland, OH: Meridian Books/World Publishing Company, 1963.

Hofstadter, Richard. *The Paranoid Style in American Politics.* New York: Alfred A. Knopf, 1965.

Holbrooke, Richard. *To End a War.* New York: Modern Library, 1998.

Howard, Albert. *An Agricultural Testament.* New York: Oxford University Press, 1943.

Huizinga, Johan. *The Waning of the Middle Ages: A Study of the Forms of Life, Thought, and Art in France and the Netherlands in the XIVth and XVth Centuries.* Garden City, NY: Doubleday Anchor Books, 1954.

Huntington, Samuel P. *The Clash of Civilizations and the Remaking of World Order.* New York: Touchstone, 1996.

Ignatieff, Michael. *The Lesser Evil: Political Ethics in an Age of Terror.* Princeton, NJ: Princeton University Press, 2004.

John Paul II. *Laborem exercens.* In *Catholic Social Thought: The Documentary Heritage,* edited by David J. O'Brien and Thomas A. Shannon. Maryknoll, NY: Orbis Books, 1992.

Johnson, Chalmers. *The Sorrows of Empire: Militarism, Secrecy, and the End of the Republic.* New York: Henry Holt and Company, 2004.

Kaplan, Robert D. *Warrior Politics: Why Leadership Demands a Pagan Ethos.* New York: Random House, 2002.

Kaveny, M. Cathleen. "Intrinsic Evil and Political Responsibility." *America: The National Catholic Weekly,* October 27, 2008.

Keegan, Robert, and William Kristol, ed. *Present Dangers: Crisis and Opportunity in American Foreign and Defense Policy.* San Francisco, CA: Encounter Books, 2000.

Kennan, George F. *American Diplomacy, 1900–1950.* New York: New Modern Library, 1951.

Kenney, Paul. *The Rise and Fall of the Great Powers.* New York: Random House, 1987.

Keynes, John Maynard. *The General Theory of Employment, Interest and Money.* New York and London: Harcourt Brace, Jovanovich, Harbinger Edition, 1964.

Kierkegaard, Søren. "The Present Age." In *A Kierkegaard Anthology,* edited by Robert Bretall. New York: Modern Library, 1936.

Koniak, Susan P. "Where Were the Lawyers? Behind the Curtain Wearing Their Magic Caps." February 6, 2002. Quoted in US Senate, *Hearing on Accountability Issues.*

Krugman, Paul. *The Conscience of a Liberal.* New York: W. W. Norton & Company, 2007.

———. *The Great Unraveling.* New York: W. W. Norton, 2003.

Lewis, Charles, and Bill Allison. *The Cheating of America.* New York: W. Morrow, 2001.

Lewis, Michael. *The Big Short: Inside the Doomsday Machine.* New York: W. W. Norton and Co., 2010.

Lincoln Savings and Loan Association v. Wall, 743 F. Supp. 901, 920 (D. D. C. 1990).

Lindblom, Charles E. "The Privileged Position of Business." Chap. 13 in *Politics and Markets.* New York: Basic Books, 1982.

Locke, John. *The Second Treatise of Government.* Indianapolis, IN: Bobbs-Merrill Company, Inc., 1952.

Lowenstein, Roger. *The End of Wall Street.* New York: Penguin Group, 2010.

———. "Triple-A Failure: How Moody's and Other Credit-Rating Agencies Licensed the Abuses That Created the Housing Bubble." *The New York Times Magazine,* April 27, 2008.

Machiavelli, Niccolò. *The Prince and the Discourses.* Translated by Luigi Ricci. New York: Random House, Inc., 1950.

MacIntyre, Alasdair. *After Virtue: A Study in Moral Theory.* Notre Dame, IN: University of Notre Dame Press, 1981.

MacNeil, Robert. *America at a Crossroad.* PBS. April 9, 2007.

Macpherson, C. B. *The Political Theory of Possessive Individualism.* Oxford, UK: Oxford University Press, 1962.

Madison, James. James Madison to William Eustis, 6 July 1819. In *Letters and Other Writings of James Madison* (Philadelphia, 1865). Quoted in Rakove, "The Perils of Originalism."

Malraux, Andre. *Man's Fate.* New York: Random House, Modern Library Edition, 1934.

Mann, James. *Rise of the Vulcans: The History of Bush's War Cabinet.* New York: Penguin Books, 2004.

Matthewes, Charles. Lecture, Clergy and Laity United for Justice and Peace, Charlottesville, VA, October 20, 2008.

May, William F. *Beleaguered Rulers: The Public Obligation of the Professional.* Louisville, KY: Westminster John Knox Press, 2001.

———. "Manichæism in American Politics." In *Witness to a Generation: Significant Writings in Christianity and Crisis (1941–1966),* edited by Wayne H. Cowan, 42–48. Indianapolis, IN: Bobbs-Merrill Company, Inc., 1966.

———. *The Physician's Covenant.* 2nd rev. ed. Louisville, KY: Westminster John Knox Press, 2000.

Mayor, Jane. *The Dark Side: The Inside Story on How the War on Terror Turned into a War on American Ideals.* New York: Doubleday, 2008.

McDonald, Forrest. *We the People: The Economic Origins of the Constitution.* Library of Conservative Thought, 1991.

McLean, Bethany, and Peter Elkind. *The Smartest Guys in the Room.* New York: Portfolio, 2003.

Melville, Herman. *Moby-Dick.* New York: Modern Library, 1930.

Menninger, Carl. *Man against Himself.* New York: Harcourt, Brace, and Company, 1938.

Miller, Richard B. "Final Draft of the Pastoral Letter." *Bulletin of the Atomic Scientists* (August–September 1983).

Miller, William Lee. *The Business of May Next: Madison and the Founding.* Charlottesville, VA: University Press of Virginia, 1992.

———. *Lincoln's Virtues: An Ethical Biography.* New York: Vintage Books, 2003.

———. *President Lincoln.* New York: Alfred A. Knopf, 2008.

Montesquieu, Baron de. *The Spirit of the Laws.* New York: Hafner Press, Macmillan Publishing Co., Inc., 1949.

Morgan, Edmund S. *American Heroes: Profiles of Men and Women Who Shaped Early America.* New York: W. W. Norton & Company, 2009.

———., ed. *Puritan Political Ideas.* Indianapolis, IN: Bobbs-Merrill Company, Inc., 1965.

National Conference of Catholic Bishops. *The Challenge of Peace: God's Promise and Our Response.* Washington, DC: United States Catholic Conference, 1983.

———. *Economic Justice for All: Pastoral Letter on Catholic Social Teaching and the U.S. Economy.* Washington, DC: United States Catholic Conference, 1986.

Niebuhr, Reinhold. *Nature and Destiny of Man.* London: Nisbet, 1941.

Nomad, Max. *Apostles of Revolution.* Boston: Little Brown, 1938.

Nye, Joseph S., Jr. *The Paradox of American Power.* New York: Oxford University Press, 2002.

Obama, Barack. "What the People Need Done: Abraham Lincoln Bicentennial." Remarks, Springfield, IL, February 12, 2009.

O'Connor, Flannery. *Mystery and Manners: Occasional Prose.* Edited by Sally Fitzgerald and Robert Fitzgerald. New York: Farrar, Straus and Giroux, 1961.

The Oxford Annotated Bible with the Apocrypha: Revised Standard Version. New York: Oxford University Press, 1965.

Packer, George. *The Assassins' Gate: America in Iraq.* New York: Farrar, Straus and Giroux, 2005.

Parker, Richard. "Government beyond Barack Obama." Review of *The Case for Big Government,* by Jeff Madrick. *New York Review of Books,* March 12, 2009

Pew Forum on Religion and Public Life. "Voting Religiously." Pew Research Center Publications, November 5, 2008. http://pewresearch.org/pubs/1022/exit-poll-analysis-religion.

Phillips, Kevin. *American Theocracy.* New York: Viking, 2006.

——. *Wealth and Democracy: A Political History of the American Rich.* New York: Broadway Books, 2002.

Pieper, Josef. *In Tune with the World: A Theory of Festivity.* New York: Harcourt, Brace and Wonk, 1965.

Pollack, Kenneth M. *The Threatening Storm: The Case for Invading Iraq.* New York: Random House, 2002.

Pollan, Michael. *The Omnivore's Dilemma.* New York: The Penguin Group, 2006.

Postman, Neil. *Amusing Ourselves to Death: Public Discourse in the Age of Show Business.* New York: Viking Penguin, 1985.

Pound, Roscoe. *The Lawyer from Antiquity to Modern Times.* St. Paul, MN: West Publishing, 1953.

Preston, Julia. "Decline Seen in Numbers of People Here Illegally." *New York Times,* July 31, 2008.

——. "An Interpreter Speaking Up for Migrants." *New York Times,* July 11, 2008.

Rakove, Jack N. "The Perils of Originalism." In Countryman, *What Did the Constitution Mean to Early Americans?*

Reich, Robert B. *Reason: Why Liberals Will Win the Battle for America.* New York: Alfred A. Knopf, 2004.

——. *The Resurgent Liberal.* New York: Random House, 1989.

——. *The Work of Nations.* New York: Vintage Books, 1992.

Ricks, Thomas E. *Fiasco: The American Military Adventure in Iraq*. New York: Penguin Press, 2006.

Robb, John. *Brave New War: The Next Stage of Terrorism and the End of Globalization*. Hoboken, NJ: John Wiley & Sons, 2007.

Rothman, Rozann. "The Impact of Covenant and Contract Theories on the Conceptions of the U.S. Constitution." *Publius* 10, no. 4 (Fall 1980).

Sampson, Anthony. *The Seven Sisters: The Great Oil Companies and the World They Shaped*. New York: Viking Press, 1975.

Savage, Charlie. *Takeover: The Return of the Imperial Presidency and the Subversion of American Democracy*. New York: Little, Brown and Company, 2007.

[Scheuer, Michael]. *Imperial Hubris*. Washington, DC: Brassey's Inc., 2004.

Schumer, Charles E., and Lindsey Graham. "The Right Way to Mend Immigration." *Washington Post*, March 19, 2010.

Shakespeare, William. *Hamlet*. In *The Complete Works of William Shakespeare*. New York: Avenel Books/Crown Publishers, Inc., 1975.

Shapiro, Ian. *Containment: Rebuilding a Strategy against Global Terror*. Princeton: Princeton University Press, 2007.

Shiller, Robert J. "Animal Spirits Depend on Trust." *Wall Street Journal*, January 27, 2009.

Skidelsky, Robert. *Keynes: The Return of the Master*. New York: Public Affairs, 2009.

Sorkin, Andrew Roth. *Too Big to Fail*. New York: Viking, 2009.

Spiegelberg, Frederic. *Living Religions of the World*. Englewood Cliffs, NJ: Prentice Hall, Inc., 1956.

Stewart, James B. *Den of Thieves*. New York: Simon & Schuster, 1991.

Suskind, Ron. *The One Percent Doctrine: Deep Inside America's Pursuit of Its Enemies Since 9/11*. New York: Simon & Schuster, 2006.

———. *The Price of Loyalty*. New York: Simon & Schuster, 2004.

Tamminen, Terry. *Lives per Gallon: The True Cost of Our Oil Addiction*. Washington, DC: Island Press, 2006.

Taylor, Charles. *The Ethics of Authenticity*. Cambridge, MA: Harvard University Press, 1991.

———. *The Sources of the Self*. Cambridge, MA: Harvard University Press, 1989.

Tett, Gillian. *Fool's Gold*. New York: Free Press, 2009.

Thurow, Lester C. *The Zero-Sum Society*. New York: Basic Books, 1980.

Tillich, Paul. *The Courage to Be*. New Haven, CT: Yale University Press, 1952.

Tocqueville, Alexis de. *Democracy in America*. Edited by J. P. Mayer. New York: Harper and Row, 1969.

Toynbee, Arnold J. *A Study of History: Abridgement of Volumes I-VI.* Edited by D. C. Somervell. New York and London: Oxford University Press, 1947.

US Senate. Committee on the Judiciary. *Hearing on Accountability Issues: Lessons Learned from Enron's Fall. Congressional Record.* 107th Congr., 2nd sess. Vol. 48.

Wallis, Jim. *God's Politics: Why the Right Gets It Wrong and the Left Doesn't Get It.* New York: Harper San Francisco, 2004.

Walter, Eugene V. *Terror and Resistance.* New York: Oxford University Press, 1972.

Weil, Simone. *The Need for Roots.* London: Routledge Kegan Paul, 1952.

Wills, Garry. "At Ease, Mr. President." *New York Times,* January 27, 2007.

Wilson, Bee. "The Last Bite: Is the World's Food System Collapsing?" *The New Yorker,* May 19, 2008.

Winthrop, John. "A Declaration in Defense of an Order of Court Made in May 1637." In Morgan, *Puritan Political Ideas,* part 2, chap. 7.

———. "A Model of Christian Charity." In Morgan, *Puritan Political Ideas,* part 2, chap. 4.

Wolin, Sheldon. *Politics and Vision.* Boston: Little, Brown and Company, Inc., 1960.

Wood, Gordon S. *The Creation of the American Republic, 1776–1787.* New York: W. W. Norton & Co., Inc., 1972.

Woodward, Bob. *State of Denial: Bush at War.* New York: Simon & Schuster, 2006.

Wright, Lawrence. *The Looming Tower: Al-Qaeda and the Road to 9/11.* New York: Alfred A. Knopf, 2007.

Yergin, Daniel, and Joseph Stanislaw. *The Commanding Heights.* New York: Simon & Schuster, 1998.

Yoo, John. *Crisis and Command: The History of Executive Power from George Washington to George W. Bush.* New York: Kaplan, 2010.

———. *The Powers of War and Peace: The Constitution and Foreign Affairs after 9/11.* Chicago: University of Chicago Press, 2005.

Zinni, Anthony. Lecture, Miller Center for the Study of the Presidency, Charlottesville, VA.

INDEX

168

Index

Fanon, Franz, 13
Faulkner, William, 128–29, 140n14
fears, runaway: and American foreign
policy, xiii–xiv, 1–25; of anarchy, 1–2,
6, 8–11, 139n3; Bush administration,
9–11, 13–14, 17, 19–21, 22; the civic
self, 22–23; Cold War containment
policy, xiii, 4–6, 140nn9–10; the
common good, 23; the conception
and exercise of power, 12–16; containment of terrorism, 11–12; containment of tyranny, 4–6; and
contractualist national identity,
xiv–xv, 83–86; curbing the imperial
presidency, 18–21; dualism, 3–4, 7,
16–17, 24–25; founders' fears, 2,
139n3; the good of order/good of social justice, 2–3, 139n4; the illusions
of empire, 17–18; limiting the imperial self, 22–23; self-containment, xiii,
5, 12, 140nn9–10; and the social
contract, 83–84, 141n16; terrorism,
6, 8–12; and tyranny, 1–2, 3–6,
139n3. *See also* anxiety
Federalist Papers, 21, 104–7
financial system collapse: boom, bubble, bust cycle, 32–33; Bush's justification for government intervention,
39–40; and claim that the market is
self-corrective, 39–40; corporate
leaders' salaries, bonuses, and stock
options, 30–31, 32, 144n6; corporate leaders' withdrawal from consequences, 31–32, 144n9; and free
market ideology, 30–33, 39–40;
Obama administration interventions, 37, 42–48; real estate market
collapse, 31, 144nn7–9; rescue and
stimulus, 37, 42–43, 45–46; securities, ratings agencies, and CDOs,
31, 144n8; stock market and real
estate bubbles, 30, 32–33; stock
market collapse, 32–33; unequal
wealth distribution and inequities
in the tax system, 32, 144n10
financial system rescue and stimulus
plan, 37, 42–43, 45–46; conservative Republican position, 46; Lincoln's long-term internal
improvements, 38, 46, 48; Obama
administration interventions, 45–48;
political costs, 47
First Amendment, xvi–xvii, 62–63
Foreign Intelligence Surveillance Act
(FISA), 19

foreign policy: Cold War containment
policy, xiii, 4–6, 140nn9–10; the conception and exercise of power, 12–16;
and runaway fears, xiii–xiv, 1–25
Founders: building system of checks
and balances, 21, 25, 45, 104–6;
containing runaway fears of tyranny
and anarchy, 2, 139n3; cultivation
of the civic self, 25; realism about
human nature, 105–6, 105–7,
151n4; and structure of government, 45, 104–6; and unitary executive theory, 21; "We the People"
and its intentions, 89–91
Frank, Robert H., 78
Freedman, Samuel G., 152n4
freedom, positive/negative, 150n2
Freedom of Information Act, 19
free market ideology in domestic policy
(bearing on other centers of power),
xiii, 49–64; and the "intermediate
institutions," 23, 58; and labor
unions, 52–55; "lean and mean"
strategies and downsizing, 53–54;
and the media, 62–64; prevailing
economic determinist analyses that
attribute income disparity to economic factors, 53–54, 146n4; the
professions of law and accounting,
49–52; and religious communities,
56–62; and the universities, 55–56
free market ideology in domestic policy
(business and government), xiii,
27–48; apologists (economic libertarians), 34–40; arguments for an autonomous free market, 35–40;
argument regarding management's
duties to stockholders, 35, 36–37; argument that the market is companion to democracy, 36, 38; argument
that the market is self-corrective, 36,
38–40; argument that the market
produces goods/commodities, 35–36,
37–38; budget and trade deficits, 28;
corporate leadership, 29–32, 33–34,
144n6, 144n9, 145n12; counter-ar-
guments, 36–40; creation of permanent underclass, 28–30, 144n2; the
evanescence of society's durable
forms, 30–33; and the financial system collapse, 30–33, 39–40,
144nn6–9; and government regulations, 34–35, 42; the Keynesian alternative (countercyclical fiscal
policies), xiii, 41–42, 79, 97; narrow-